WHY FISH BITE—
AND WHY THEY DON'T

is hotly debated from Maine to Alaska, from the swamps of Louisiana to the shores of California. But whether you are channel fishing for flounder, surf casting for stripers, or lake trolling for smallmouth bass, here is an entirely different kind of guide to the art and science of fishing in fresh or salt water.

What makes it different?

Dr. James Westman applies his scientific knowledge of fish to catching them. From theory to practice, from practice to perfection, successful methods are culled from his varied experience of more than 20 years in the study of species, their habits and their habitats. For example, he tells why fish are sensitive to sounds, smells and tastes; why they migrate to water levels of varying temperatures; how they feed and where they spawn.

Here, in entertaining style rich with fishing lore and anecdotes, he describes the techniques of fishing in lakes, ponds, rivers, streams and oceans; explains the lures, lines and bait to be used; points up little-known facts about the art of angling in deep waters or marshy lands.

The difference, then, is a complete book on fishing that looks at both ends of the line—the fish as a whole and the fisherman who, by knowing his challenger, catches his fish.

THE AUTHOR

James Westman, who holds a Ph.D. in Biology, writes a column for several New Jersey newspapers, and is Chairman, Department of Wild Life, Rutgers University. Also, he is an active member of seven scientific and conservation societies, including The Outdoor Writers Association of America, the New York Academy of Sciences, and The American Fisheries Society.

Illustrations by Ray Ingham

WHY FISH BITE
and
WHY THEY DON'T

by

James Westman

drawings by
Ray Ingham

1974 EDITION

Published by

WILSHIRE BOOK COMPANY

12015 Sherman Road

No. Hollywood, California 91605

Telephone: (213) 875-1711

Printed by

HAL LEIGHTON PRINTING CO.
P. O. Box 1231
Beverly Hills, California 90213
Telephone: (213) 346-8500

Library of Congress Catalog Card Number 61-10318
Printed in the United States of America.

Wilshire Book Company edition
is published by special arrangement
with Prentice-Hall, Inc., Englewood Cliffs, N. J.
ISBN 0-87980-261-8

To Ginger

Contents

Contents

WHY FISH BITE
AND WHY THEY DON'T

Prologue: Consider a Boy With A Fishing Rod....

Consider a boy with a fishing rod and a can of worms as he heads for a nearby pond or river, afoot or on a bicycle. Imbued by the spirit of research and an eagerness for adventure, he is about to engage in an activity that is nearly as old as Man: "What lurks in the deep pool at the bend of the river, and how can I catch it?"

Science, with all its shelves of books, pamphlets, and treatises on the classification, life histories, population dynamics and management of fishes has almost entirely ignored this question about why fish bite in the first place! Perhaps the scientists have been too busy studying the less obvious mysteries about fish. Perhaps they, too, have taken an answer for granted and have become victims of tradition and dictated fashions. Or perhaps they have felt understandably embarrassed about being conspicuous with hook and line studies while operating on state or federal funds. The fact remains, nevertheless, that fishery biologists have been professionally more interested in fishes than in fishing—that fascinating and mysterious relationship between man and his underwater quarry . . .

Once before the boy had seen the big fish in the deep pool at the bend of the river. He had been peering down into the dark water under the tree root and had seen the great shadowy form undulating gently with the current. He had guided the worm down near the shadow, but the big fish had only moved away slowly —farther up under the bank.

This time the monster came out of his lair and leisurely followed the worm for a foot or two as it was being slowly retrieved, only to turn back suddenly. The boy was momentarily stunned by the size of the great fish and by its unblinking eyes and deliberate movement. He had never seen or expected anything like it, and he felt his scalp and the roof of his mouth tighten and tingle as if charged with electricity, and his heart begin to pound violently up near the base of his throat. When the spasm had subsided, he noticed that his heart continued to beat rapidly and that he was possessed with an uncontrollable trembling and sweating. His head began to ache.

He fished for a full hour more, but saw and felt nothing. He began to feel let down and a bit frustrated. When he had told his Uncle Charlie about the big fish many days ago, Uncle Charlie had put his hand on his shoulder and had told him that it was all a matter of luck and patience. But he had tried and tried, and what could he do? Fish eat, but this huge one had been given fresh worms again and again, and wasn't much interested. Was he always to be the unlucky fisherman?

The boy pulled up his line and cleaned the hook preparatory to going home. Glancing into the worm can, he saw that there was only one small, stretched-out worm in the crusted bottom dirt. It was partly broken and didn't smell so good, so—almost mechanically—he emptied the can and rinsed it in the river.

Only then did he begin to relive his recent experience and feel a mounting inner excitement. Next time he would be more careful in his approach and he would hook the worm differently. And he would try small frogs, and grasshoppers, and one of those "water lizards"! After all, Uncle Charlie didn't catch big fish like this in the river. Uncle Charlie always went away somewhere with someone to catch them.

The boy had never before experienced an attack of buck fever and he wondered what it was. He wasn't going to say anything about it, not even to Uncle Charlie.

Someone once said that all children are born with the spirit of research, but that it is spanked out of most by the age of seven. While this conclusion may be an overstatement, we must admit that the spirit of research does suffer a bit during the early years from such things as parental fears, methods of teaching, and demands for conformity. But the spirit often becomes only latent, and like Sleeping Beauty in the fable, is ready to be awakened by the right kiss of circumstance. The sounds of the surf and the crying gulls, the quiet surface of a lake, the scent of pine needles and wet autumn leaves, or the smell of smoke and the glow of a crackling fire —all these mysteries are of the music of Nature that can awaken and keep us among the truly living.

During the years, our own researches into the phenomena of why fish bite, and why they don't, have been met with mixed reactions. Some persons have condoned them as invaluable contributions to progress in fishery management; others have been skeptical; while still others have scorned or condemned them as dealing with a subject unworthy of science or scientists (as one colleague put it: "How low can you get?"). It remained for a newspaper editor, however, to terminate a comment with the entreaty: "Isn't *anything* sacred anymore?"

We have no desire to enter into controversy over the possible merits or demerits of our researches. We simply believe that the spirit of the boy with his fishing rod and can of worms, far from requiring any apologia, is something that should be understood, shared, and encouraged by all of us.

The child is still the father and the leader of the man.

James Westman
Hampton, N. J.

Why Jim Westman Fishes

by A. H. Underhill, Director, Div. Fish & Game,
New Jersey

It has been said that fishing is a contemplative not a competitive sport. This is only partially true. There are certain kinds of competition between fishermen, and there is very real competition between fishermen and fish. In this book, Dr. Westman delves into some of the mysteries of these relationships.

The small boy challenged and baffled by the monster trout in the old swimming hole has never lost that "heart in the mouth" feeling! More important, despite the disciplines of a brilliant scientific career, Dr. Westman has never lost the questioning, boyish enthusiasm that society all too soon regiments out of most of us.

Jim Westman had to write this book. All of us who fish or who just enjoy fine writing are richer for that compulsion. In a series of delightfully written chapters he calls on a vast store of scientific knowledge and practical fishing experience to answer the perennial questions of why fish bite and why they don't. There are many good fishery biologists; some of them are good fishermen; a very few are good writers. I know of no one who blends these attributes as admirably as does Dr. Westman.

His reputation as a scientist has long been established. This book demonstrates his skill as a writer. It would appear to be my pleasant duty to recall some twenty odd years of professional and personal association and authenticate his right to speak as an angler.

Jim Westman fishes to catch fish. He almost always succeeds! When ordinary methods fail, the reason becomes as important as the most complicated scientific experiment, and the answer is sought in much the same way. An orange head on a fluke spinner, a red and yellow bucktail trolled in the propeller wash for smallmouth, a certain twist in presenting a fly to a sophisticated brown produce fish in the pan while others are still blaming the moon or the water temperature. These successful techniques are developed through enthusiasm, imagination, love of fishing, and scientific training. Throughout the years the key has been an inquiring mind that has refused to accept the conventional approach.

Trolling lakes in Canada, chumming blues on the Ridge, plugging largemouth at Sodus or coaxing stripers out of Cape Cod Canal, these same qualities have emerged. Why fish don't bite becomes a challenge. After the gauntlet is picked up and the dust of battle clears, Dr. Westman has usually stored away another anecdote for *Why Fish Bite*. . . .

1   The Incomplete Angler

*The problem of ignorance is
not so much a lack of knowledge as in knowing so many
things that just ain't so.*

—Author Unknown

Fishermen have long been regarded as a special breed
of humanity deserving of particular compassion and
indulgence. They are wont to be portrayed as big-
hearted, naive, blustering and rather clumsy fellows
whose whims must be catered to from time to time.

Actually this is a gross oversimplification of the
case, although perhaps a convenient one, because there
are many sorts of fishermen. There are generous and
selfish ones; the simple and the sophisticated; the intelligent and the stupid; the thoughtful and the thought-
less; the vociferous and the quiet; the awkward and the
graceful. They come from all walks of life and can be
male or female; introverts or extroverts; "purists" or
"meat hunters"; vegetarians or gourmets.

The motives that prompt individuals to go fishing
are equally varied. Some persons wish only to get outdoors to relax, and use angling equipment as an excuse
or prop for the occasion. Others are motivated by the

competitive urge in one form or other, or perhaps by the anticipation of some very fresh fish cooked gently to a turn with a further supply in the deep freeze. Still others find in angling a means to explore and appreciate the mysteries of Nature, including its eternal mystery of beauty. Very often it is some combination of these or other motives.

Obviously, this question of motive in angling is of primary importance to the catching of fish: An angler who is satisfied with sun and outdoor exercise will hardly put in the effort of one who wants to catch fish above all else; nor will the angler who insists upon catching fish by one method only catch as many as an angler who can and will use any method that is the most timely and effective. This calls for a bit of honest soul searching on the part of the angler. What interests him most? Fishing? Catching fish? Meat fishing? Competition? Exploring Nature? Relaxing? Making lures? Club activity? Achievement? Escape? Peace of mind? What?

It is this wide variety of human interests and involvements that makes angling such a unique and paradoxical sport. What other sport, for example, is so completely dominated by millions of amateurs? What other pays so little attention to professional knowledge, or has such little professional knowledge made available to it? And in what other sport do the ablest or most advanced participants—the "pros" as it were—shun contests, retire into a world of their own, and spend much money on their sport rather than receive much from it? Is it small wonder that fishermen are often considered to be "crazy or something"?

Actually, all this makes sense if we realize that angling, in its highest form, is a contemplative sport rather than a contest among persons. There are fishing tournaments, contests and pools, to be sure, but the greatest competitions and challenges in angling are personal matters and more like those to be found in the pursuit of an art or a science. This is why many of the great artists in fishing—the counterparts of the professionals in other sports—are little if at all known and live in a world apart. It is often an unbelievable or conveniently deniable world for those who have not glimpsed it, but it exists and will continue to do so, despite all skepticism.

Needless to say these "professionals" or complete anglers are not just the masters of one form of angling, but of all forms. Dry fly, wet fly, bait casting, bait fishing, trolling—whatever the occasion demands in fresh or salt water—they have the "know how" and are quick to apply it. They spend years studying the habits and behavior of fishes; they seek out the latest scientific findings, manufacture many of their own lures, and frequently employ methods that are completely unknown to incomplete anglers. Why do they do it? Probably for the same reason that the inveterate mountain climber responds to greater and greater challenges—simply "because it is there".

We believe that many of the millions of incomplete anglers would like to pursue their interest much further, have a look into the private world of the "pros" and, meanwhile, gain a greater appreciation of that world we call "The Outdoors". So let us examine this problem of fishing from many angles and attempt, first of all, to appraise some of the more prevalent concepts, weaknesses and strengths of the incomplete angler.

I.

If there are any common denominators or failings characteristic of anglers—or trends toward same—they are:

1. A gullibility and inconsistency that can put even a fish to shame.

2. An insistence upon catching the fish on his (the angler's) terms, rather than those of the fish.

This gullibility and stubbornness, observations have shown, are not only largely responsible for the failures and frustrations of the fisherman but, in consequence of these failures and frustrations, for attitudes and actions that can be truly amazing. A dry fly purist, for example, may throw up his hands in horror at the mere thought of chumming a trout pool but may be the first to take full advantage of nature's handout in the form of a "hatch" of aquatic insects. Or he may take great care in spraying his No. 10 Irresistible or his No. 18 Black Gnat with the latest in silicone sprays so that it will float correctly, only to spend more time later trying to get legislation passed that will prevent his wet fly brethren from including any weighting material in the construction of their nymphs or wet flies so that they will sink properly.

Other anglers may translate their frustrations or fondness of self-delusion into the purchase of more and more lures (often much more effective in catching fishermen than fish), or into various attempts actually to legislate the fish onto their hooks, sometimes with serious consequences.

One of the most extreme examples of this angler frustration and its results is afforded by the striped bass, *Roccus saxatilus*, of the Atlantic coast of the United States. This abundant food and game fish is largely a species of the great estuaries and tidal rivers such as Chesapeake Bay, Delaware Bay, and the lower Hudson River. Some of the bass of these populations migrate, however, and hundreds of thousands of them move up the coast during the spring months and return again in the fall to winter in the more southern estuaries of their range.

Even though the species is far more available and catchable to salt water anglers during these migrations than at other times, the "striper" is perhaps the most difficult of all food and game fishes to locate successfully and to entice onto the hook. (Exception: the muskellunge or "muskie".) Indeed, during the summer months, successful striper angling is almost entirely a matter of "know-how" and skill that is possessed by only a tiny minority of salt water anglers. And even these tight-lipped experts, who lurk under bridges and around pilings and other "hot spots" in the darkness of the night, seldom fish the striper with great confidence. Some unskilled anglers actually try for years without catching a striped bass.

The result of this lack of cooperation on the part of the striper is that the angling efforts for the species on the Atlantic coast make but a small, if any, dent in the harvestable supplies of this fishery resource or, for that matter, in what probably should be harvested for good conservation. Contrary to popular belief, nearly all fish and other animal populations *must* be harvested up to a point if increased productivity is to be realized. The principle is the same as for the asparagus bed. The asparagus *must* be cut if more is to be produced.

Yet it is doubtful if any other species of fish comes in for more effort, on the part of special angler interests, to have it completely reserved for their purposes only. These attempts to legislate the fish onto the hooks by seeking to ban all netting, spearing and "snatching" of the species have been variously termed "social legislation," "political grab legislation," "political football," etc.; and unfortunately, attempts to gain realistic and sound compromises in the situation have almost always failed regardless of the sincerity and good will behind such endeavors. A consequence of the situation can be seen in the following:

"During the past 30 years there has been a growing trend towards 'social' legislation in the marine fisheries of the several Atlantic states. Except in rare instances, such social legislation seeks to protect one particular fishery interest at the expense of another, or others, and in some instances seeks a monopoly for the particular interest.

"At least four immediate results from this 'social' legislation have become apparent:

1. The legislation may damage one type of fishery without any measurable gain to the faction responsible for the legislation.
2. The legislation may tend to be nullified—indeed

its desired effect reversed—by the laws of other states.

3. The fishes are unable to read the law books and therefore cannot comply with the legislation.

4. It may result in needless waste—social, economic, and biological." *

Beneath all these attitudes and actions on the part of the angler, there seems to be a tendency to believe that the numbers of fish caught accurately reflect the quantities of fish in the water. And since careful scientific studies by many persons over the years have repeatedly shown that a small minority of anglers nearly always catches the majority of fish that are taken, is it small wonder that Mr. John Doe Angler may conclude "scarcity" and wish to do something about it in the name of "conservation"?

* From Twelfth Annual Report, 1953, of Atlantic States Marine Fisheries Commission to the Congress of the United States and to the Governors and Legislators of the Fifteen Compacting States.

Actually, other scientific studies have revealed that the quantity of a species of game fish in the water very often has little to do with the number Mr. John Doe Angler catches; and still further scientific researches have shown some of the reasons why. But "J. D." is very often a busy man who seeks relaxation in his fishing, and justifiably so. Usually he doesn't wish to knock himself out with intellectual activity, or physical activity —much less both—in order to catch fish. It may be much easier and far more pleasant to spend evenings at the rod and gun club, deplore conditions, and prescribe actions for others ostensibly to remedy the situation. Indeed, the means—this club activity—can sometimes become the end, and it often makes little difference whether or not the prescriptions are antiquated "snake remedies" that have been demonstrated again and again to be ineffective, if not mathematically ridiculous, or whether or not such insistence is a source of embarrassment to the more thoughtful club members.

Another interesting trend in angling—and one that seems to have become increasingly popular during recent years—is a lack of interest in keeping the fish for eating purposes. The animal is returned to the water, often with the comment (and we sometimes suspect a pointed one) "I don't like eating fish, I return every fish I catch to the water!"

Here, it would seem, is the ultimate in angler sophistication and unselfishness. Yet some years ago we observed one such angler participating in a tuna tournament (rampant in the uniform of his club) which resulted in tons of tuna spoiling in the hot sun while

the judges counted and weighed them. Needless to say, such denials of the flesh, and affectations of *pour le sport* can leave something to be desired.

Actually, the apparent, increasing loss of interest in the eating of fish as a part of the angling ritual, seems to coincide with our ever present "busyness" and a decreasing art of cookery in the home. In other words, if a species of fish tastes good when fried quickly and without much care, it is a "good eating" fish. If, on the other hand, it does not respond to such treatment, it is a "poor eating" fish. Such attributes as texture and delicacy of the flesh now seem all but unknown. Quick frying, before or after freezing, now seems to be the sole criterion for the edibility of one of the principal foods of Man!

Not long ago, less than a century in fact, the carp was generally considered to be an excellent game fish and table delicacy. Successful efforts were made, through the Congress of the United States, to stock it in many fresh waters of the nation. It still is an excellent game fish and table delicacy for those who know how to catch and prepare it; but to most persons it is an ugly, tasteless trash fish, and is unjustifiably accused of being a "spawn eater" and a fiendish competitor of bass and other "game" species.

The catfish, one of the tastiest of all fresh water fishes and one that bites best during the caressing darkness of a soft summer night, is easy to clean and prepare by those who know how; but is now neglected by the majority of anglers in many areas. Even the lowly lamprey, which is not a "true" fish, was once considered a table delicacy by epicures:

"Then a lamprey in a sauce of shrimps was brought in on a platter. Seeing this, the host remarked, 'It was caught while gravid. If caught after spawning, its meat is inferior. Here is the recipe for the sauce: Oil of the first extraction from (the town of) Venafrum; roe from the Spanish mackerel; native wine five years old added while the sauce is simmering—in fact Chian is the most suitable for cooking—white pepper, and vinegar from Lesbian wine. I was the first to show how to blend in green rockets and bitter elecampane. Curtillis says to add un-

washed sea-urchins, for the shellfish's natural brine is better than any processed salt." *

But enough of these negative traits of anglers, or those which contribute to lost weekends! What of those characteristics that keep the angler an eternal optimist and which can offer him the keys of the kingdom?

II.

Of all the urges that motivate us to go fishing, the competitive urge, in one form or another, is perhaps the paramount one. We visualize the big lunker in the pool, the big score at sea, the spot in the lake, or the shadowed mysteries of the gorge. Or perhaps we are prompted to "beat George", or win the pool, or set a record. In any case, the invitation and the challenge are there—beckoning yet indifferent.

This competitive urge can take on some bizarre aspects at times. A number of years ago, for instance, two well-known big game anglers were standing on the dock of an elite yacht club on Long Island earnestly conversing about a porgy (scup) fishing trip—a sport generally considered to be quite plebian and a mere matter of sinker-bouncing and meat-hunting. Two neophytes were standing nearby and were so astonished by the famous anglers' concern with porgy fishing that they were prompted to ask about it.

"Ah, my friends," replied one of the gentlemen, "I can see that you have never engaged in competitive porgy

*. . . HORACE, Second Book of Satire, No. 8.

fishing. It's five dollars a porgy and when you're five porgies down, man how you can fish!" (We should quickly advise that there is a surplus of porgies in the sea.)

Sometimes the competitive urge takes on a negative or "show me" aspect. Not long ago, one of the deans of the Maine guides—we shall call him "George" and not by his right name—was fishing a middle-aged party for landlocked salmon. (We shall refer to her as "Mrs. J."). It was a fairly good day for salmon and "Mrs. J." hooked a number of fish, through George's knowledge, only to lose all of them because of her insistence upon playing them on her own terms. Her failures, of course, were blamed upon a number of circumstances, but usually upon George.

This went on all day. Finally, late in the afternoon, "Mrs. J." hooked a fine fish in the five-pound class and succeeded in holding it, despite unforgivable mistakes, until the salmon reached the boat and turned on its side in the 'possum act that landlocks frequently put on. "Mrs. J." was just putting down her rod in a "now let George do it" manner, when the salmon exploded from the water and landed in the boat at George's feet.

Perhaps "Mrs. J." didn't realize the hard time she had been giving George all day, because George just automatically grabbed the salmon and threw it back into the water with the statement, "Now bring that fish in right."

By far the most rewarding forms of competition in angling are those which take place between the fish and the angler and within the angler himself. This is particularly true when angling becomes a means to explore and appreciate the beauty and mystery of Nature, because the search for truth is in itself a form of competition that can be at once humbling, rewarding, and memorable. When exploring the outdoors, for instance, and meanwhile gaining knowledge and appreciation, the angler is actually exploring the mystery of life itself to which he feels himself both drawn and attached. This is the profound, but most intriguing aspect of angling and the one that is most difficult to explain. It is involved with the spirit of the boy with the fishing rod and can of worms, whom we described earlier and with the spirit and feeling of Man that motivates him to silent prayer and the giving of thanks.

Perhaps we can best convey what we mean here by quoting the words of a veteran angler who was moved to write them at the passing of his friend and professional predecessor. The words are now cast in a bronze tablet on a rock beside a swiftly flowing trout stream where the stream winds its way through a deep and densely wooded gorge. Near the height of a late spring or summer day, shafts of sunlight will sometimes find the bronze tablet and illuminate the words for those who may be there and who may wish to read:

> *"When mist and shadows rob pool and run*
> *of shape and substance,*
> *When the voice of the wood thrush stills*
> *and the dog trout shakes his lethargy,*
> *We will remember stalwart, gentle master*
> *of the angler's art,*
> *Half submerged in the smother,*
> *Unerringly shooting that long line,*
> *watchfully mending the drift.*
> *Nevermore will your skilled hand tempt*
> *the patriarchs of the flood.*
> *Farewell old timer."* *

When the potential blessings of angling are counted and weighed, it becomes obvious that they cannot be gained from any recipe book and do-it-yourself kit. Too much is involved. But to the angler who will search for truth with all his faculties, and who will not rebel when truth becomes stranger than fiction, all these blessings are obtainable. He can also become a master angler with unlimited horizons, and will be able to approach any fishing waters, anywhere, with a comforting measure of confidence. Even that very old and wary bass in the cove, for instance, will have numbered

---

* By Henry Schaefer.

days, because, as Don Schulte, another angler, once put it:

"On some morning when mist hides the water, or an evening all shot with sunset, he will catch him, too."

2

The Fish In Person

. . . that class of vertebrate animals which lives exclusively in water, breathes through gills, and whose limbs take the form of fins.
—Encyclopaedia Britannica

Many thousands of pages have been written about the biology of fishes—their shapes, colorations, physiologies, life histories, etc. While much of this knowledge is of little, if any, practical value to the catching of fish, some of it can be of invaluable assistance. Our immediate task, then, is briefly to describe those biological characteristics of fishes which we have found to be of greatest value during angling safaris. Let us consider these characteristics and indicate why each one is, or can be, a very important thing to know about.

SIGHT

The "fishy eye" is something that should never be either underestimated or overestimated despite the fact that some people eat fish eyes (and we're not referring to tapioca pudding).

In the first place, nearly all fishes are able to see objects above the water and at an angle, depending upon the depth of the fish in the water, the distance away, and the height of the object. The turbidity of the water, the condition of the surface (whether smooth or broken) and the amount of light, are also important factors. In the second place, most fish can see underwater objects at considerable distances, depending again upon such factors as turbidity and the amount of light, and have really keen sight when the object is quite close. In fact some species can detect a 4X leader (monofilament) in clear water and moderate light, while certain other species apparently can see well at night or in the gloom of deep water. Here there may be some confusion as to the chief means of detection. In other words, does the fish actually see a moving object under conditions of near total darkness, or detect it from a flight path, vibrations, or from a combination of these? (We have often asked ourselves this question when catching fish on artificial lures in deep water after sundown.)

The nocturnal habits of certain fishes are sometimes suggested by the large, owl-like pupils of their eyes. The pike-perches (walleye, blue pike, and sauger), the snook, *Centropomus undecimalis*, of Florida and the Gulf states, and the silver hake, or whiting, *Merluccius* sp., are good examples.

The fact that many other fishes have big eyes and are not known to be creatures of the night suggests some interesting possibilities. For example, the common cisco or lake "herring", *Coregonus artedii*, of the Great Lakes drainage has a suspiciously large eye. This

deep water "cousin" of the whitefish can often be taken
in numbers by angling at certain times of year, by
those who know how, and some experiments in night
fishing might be worthwhile.

Salt water fishes often have the aid of organic lighting or "fire" in the water. This fire comes from myriads
of tiny plants and animals, called *plankton,* and from
certain larger planktonic animals such as jellyfishes and
"sea walnuts." When disturbed, these organisms flash
like fireflies in the darkness until the disturbed water
glows with a phosphorescent hue.

Sometimes this organic "fire" can be spectacularly
beautiful, as when fishing for snappers in the Gulf
Stream at night or when chumming for bluefish off the
New Jersey coast. We recall such an occasion a few
years ago while bluefishing at New Jersey's famed
Shrewsbury Rocks. . . .

It was a hot, muggy night, despite a brisk wind out
of the southwest, and the darkness seemed to be closing
in on the lurching skiff and its white light from the
gasoline lantern hung on a pole amidships. Flashes of
heat lighting were playing the horizons and would
momentarily silhouette the distant shores.

Within the circle of light cast by the lantern the
heaving water was clear and blue. One could see the
chum of freshly ground menhaden drifting away from
the boat out into the mysterious black water where the
baited hooks had been cast. Soon a glowing spot appeared in the dark water, and then another and another.
A six-pound "blue" struck savagely at one of the baits
and the action had begun. Within minutes the black

sea outside the circle of artificial light began to blossom with glowing patches and comet-like streaks of phosphorescent light. The four anglers in the open skiff—their backs bare except for the straps of their Neoprene fishing pants over their shoulders—began to sweat with the labor of meeting the onslaught with light tackle. By now the bluefish were within the circle of light and one could see them prowling savagely around the boat.

Some ten minutes later, large, slow-moving streaks of light appeared in the dark water. These were ground sharks slowly moving in on the melee, and we glanced at our friend Captain Otto with the faint hope that he might be too tired to catch one. In vain. "Cap" was already preparing his little shark rod, with a gleam in his eye. Soon, shark blood, chum, sharks, bluefish, the streaks of "fire", the wind and the flashes of lightning all became part of an extravaganza with the tossing skiff and its gasoline lantern at the center of the stage. We stopped fishing just to sit down and observe this spectacle of Nature's wonderland.

The working angles and distances at which a fish can see objects above the water can be illustrated by some simple diagrams. The principle involved here is the refraction, or bending, of light at the surface of the water, and this refraction has two very important results. First of all, it makes the fish appear to be farther out from us than it actually is and, in turn, makes us appear higher up than we actually are, to the fish. Secondly, this refraction phenomenon limits the area of surface— or "window"—through which the fish can see objects above the water.

Seeing a fish in the water where it isn't is nothing new to most of us. We know, for example, that when we poke a stick, or our fishing rod, into the water, it appears to bend where the water meets the air. Further —if we have perhaps attempted to shoot carp with a bow and arrow—we know we must aim at a point "this side" of the carp and not where we see it.

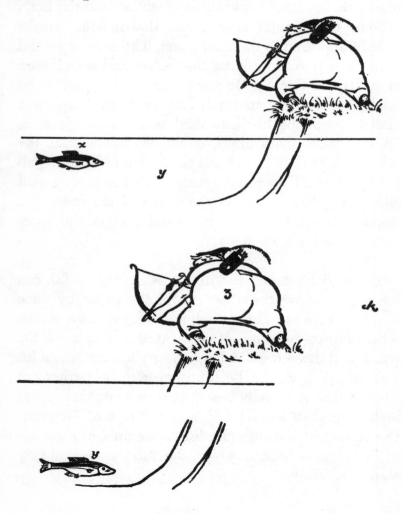

The bowman in Figure 1 (who is obviously very expert in these matters) is aiming at Position "y", where the fish actually is, rather than at Position "x", where he sees the fish. Meanwhile, the fish, which is really at Position "y", sees the bowman at Position "z", rather than where the archer really is at Position "k".

Now that all of us may be convinced, confused, or frustrated, we can consider Figure 2, which illustrates the phenomenon of the "surface window". Actually this is a very important phenomenon, because it explains why we may wish to crouch down a bit when fishing, particularly in a stream containing wild trout (big ones).

The size of the surface window, through which the fish can see objects above the water, is apparently governed by (1) a fixed angle, and (2) the distance of the fish below the surface. Such factors as turbidity, amount of light, and the condition of the surface are again important.*

Sometimes these careful calculations can be upset by mirages. In other words, the fish can occasionally see us even if we are beyond his horizon. This can be very disturbing at times, particularly when trout fishing, and not enough is known about the lighting conditions that produce it. It usually happens, however, when standing against the sky or without an immediate background and casting under tree branches or into the shade of some other type of overhang. Even at near

---

* To those readers who may wish to go into this matter and other related subjects more deeply, we suggest they read Dr. Brian Curtis's delightful book entitled: "The Life Story of the Fish, His Morals and Manners." Harcourt, Brace, & Co., N. Y.

darkness trout can be "spooked" at almost unbelievable distances under such circumstances.

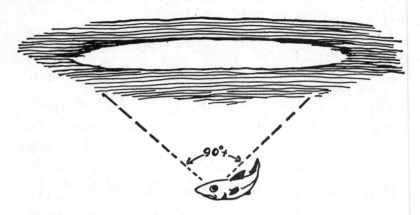

Can fish distinguish colors?

This question is frequently asked despite—or perhaps because of—the great emphasis on color in so many fish lures. For there are many factors that can confuse observations on color perception in fishes, and thoughtful anglers have realized this. In the first place there is the problem of compensating for different degrees of *brilliance* and *saturation* of colors in underwater tests, as well as for the *hues* of these colors. In the second place there are the factors of shape and movement of the colored test objects underwater. Finally, there is the important matter of previous experiences—or preconditioning—of the fishes used in an experiment.

Despite all these difficulties, it has been scientifically demonstrated that at least some species can distinguish certain colors, and that there may be an order of preference for these colors. Smallmouth and largemouth bass, for example, usually show preference for red and for yellow, although there seems to be considerable doubt about these fishes' ability to distinguish red from certain shades of purple.

Actually, much scientific research remains to be done on this matter of color perception in fishes. Meanwhile it is very profitable to keep in mind the three attributes of color—*brilliance, hue,* and *saturation*—and presume that the fish is sensitive to all three.

HEARING AND FEELING

These two senses are considered together, because it is not known just where one ends and the other begins in fishes—or for that matter how much the two may overlap. Together, however, they represent one of the most remarkable capacities possessed by any animal in the world (including humans), and this is why fishes are often considered to possess a sixth sense. Needless to say, it is very important for a fisherman to know something about this sixth sense, because it can work to both his advantage and disadvantage.

Perhaps we should begin by pointing out that hearing and feeling are two means of detecting vibrations. We humans, for instance, detect some vibrations (sound) through our ears, and others through our sense of touch. Sometimes we are aware of both hearing and feeling vibrations, as when a big organ is played in a church, or when a fog horn lets go at sea.

Unlike humans, however, most fishes have a special mechanism in addition to their ears for detecting vibrations. Not only this, but they live in a medium (water) which conducts vibrations much more rapidly and efficiently than air. The result? Fishes are highly sensitive to vibrations. Indeed certain species have been discovered to detect sound vibrations up to 20,000 frequencies per second (attention, Hi-Fi enthusiasts) while others have been found capable of distinguishing a half-tone interval in our musical scale!

Now before we become too alarmed about this and start thinking about insulating our boats and canoes with soundproof material, it should be pointed out that fish grow up in a veritable bedlam of natural noises and are apt not to pay much attention to some new vibration unless—and this is very important—they associate it with danger or something very attractive. (We will have occasion to discuss this vital matter of "learning" from experience very shortly). Actually, the quiet lake that we find so restful and refreshing is an auditory mirage. For as one team of investigators * has described it:

"The volume of sound to which fish are constantly subjected is almost unbelievable. Until one has had the opportunity to listen to the natural noises in a lake, it is difficult to realize the noise level which can be attained."

For those who may be interested in anatomical matters—or in how the fish can be such a sensitive creature—a very brief explanation may suffice. The so-called *lateral line* on the sides of most fishes is actually a series of pits or openings in the skin and scales of the animal. Behind these openings, and in the body of the fish, there runs a nerve in a sort of sheath or tube. Under each

---

* Henry F. Moore and H. William Newman.

opening of the scale a tiny branch from this nerve
extends. In other words, when we touch this *lateral line,*
we almost rub the raw nerves of the fish, and it obviously
makes little difference which way we rub them! It is
believed by some that this special mechanism also
serves as a type of sonar to enable the fish to detect
objects quickly and without having to see them.

Lest this *lateral line* be not enough, fish have ears.
We don't see these ears from the outside, but when we
dissect the head of a fish, there they are, in "capsules",
at each side of the brain!

Then, of course, the swim bladder in some fishes is
connected to their ears through a special organ called
the *Webberian ossicles* and acts as an additional auditory organ. These Webberian ossicles are in turn—but
shall we quit while we're ahead?

It is at this point in our discussion of the sense of
hearing—feeling in fishes that something should be said
about the ancient art of guddling, or catching fish with

the bare hands by stroking their bellies and then grab-
bing them suddenly. Old pros, Scotsmen, and certain
others are apt to know about guddling, but may not
admit it because lawmakers seem at least to have heard
of it and have seldom included the method as one of
the legal means for catching fresh water fishes.

Persons well experienced in the art of guddling—
and many do it just for fun and throw the fish back—
are well aware of the lateral line in fishes and take
great pains not to touch the sides of their quarry. Sometimes this can be a problem, as one of our guddle-wise
friends discovered one day when the temptations and
circumstances of the moment proved to be too much
for him. His confession, some years later, was not heard
in any sacred circumstances—in fact it was tape recorded at a New Year's Eve party—and can be reported
here with his permission. Here is a reasonable facsimile
with names changed (in this case to protect both the
innocent and the guilty):

"You remember, folks, that our son George was at
the training base up there and you know that this base
is right near where we catch those giant rainbow trout
in the spring of the year. Well, we went up to visit
George—my wife, daughter, and I—and after having
a wonderful visit with him we decided to look over the
old territory. It was just before the opening of the trout
season and we had the streams to ourselves. It was shirt-
sleeve weather and the hot sun was melting the remains
of the winter snows. You could even sense its white
heat breathing life into the gray-brown wood of the

shrubs and trees, and everything seemed about ready to burst forth.

"The streams were in beautiful condition, and as my daughter Jane and I walked them, we saw the tail of a rainbow trout in almost every hole. Then, suddenly, we saw the most gigantic trout tail we had ever seen—up under some brush at the edge of a large pool. Remember, the trout season had not opened and we had no rod. Yet here was a giant rainbow trout symbolizing the spring of the year and some other things. You know the old saying about how a young man's fancy turns to certain thoughts at this time. Well, an older man's fancy does this too, but it also turns to other related matters, and here I was gazing at this—this magnificent spectacle under the brush at the edge of the pool!

"Well, to make a long story short, I stationed Jane at the lower riffle of the pool. Then I took off my shoes and trousers and walked slowly into the icy water, toward the underbrush at the far side of the pool. My feet and legs became numbed with the cold almost at once, but my approach was successful and I reached down into the water and slowly, up under the overhanging brush. Suddenly, I felt a belly.

"Doc, this was no ordinary belly. It was a tremendous belly—the biggest I had ever felt—and I knew I couldn't get any kind of a quick grip to heave the fish out, so I just stroked his belly for a while, thinking about what to do next. As expected, the big fish didn't mind this a bit and just moved up and down slightly as I stroked him. I began to move my hand forward, very gradually, with the idea of trying to grab his head. Finally, just as I reached his throat, I grabbed and lifted all in one motion. I missed, and the fish showered me with ice water as it took off and swam madly around the pool. But it came back up under the brush, and after I had cleared my eyes and stopped shivering a bit, I went after him again. This time I must have touched his lateral line or come near to it, because he took off almost at once, showering me with ice water again, and tearing madly around the pool. But he returned to the hole under the brush, probably because that was the only place to hide. I began to feel that I might be able to outlast this monster.

"These events were repeated again and again until I was drenched with ice water and shaking like a leaf. I couldn't see very well and it was all I could do to keep my right hand from trembling when I started to guddle the fish. But I kept on with it.

"Finally, I couldn't find the fish when I groped under the brush. I looked around. And there was Jane gazing at a beautiful eight-pound rainbow flopping on the beach at the side of the riffle. All I could think, in my half paralyzed condition, was 'Well done thou good and faithful daughter. This one's for the oven!'"

SMELL AND TASTE

Fish have a well developed sense of smell and make use of it in a number of ways that are of importance to the angler. Indeed, it is apparently through odor perception that species such as salmon are able to locate the rivers of their birth after spending a year, or years, at sea.

Of great interest to the angler is the fact that fish not only can detect various odors, but also give off certain odors that can be detected by other fish. Bass, for example, can tell water in which minnows have been recently present; and in like manner the minnows can detect the recent presence of a predator fish. Perhaps of even greater interest is the fact that at least some fishes, when frightened, give off a *fear substance* and that the odor of this fear substance can be detected by other fishes.

It has been scientifically demonstrated that at least some fishes can detect human odor and are repelled by it. It is not known just how extensive this detection of human odor is in fishes, but it's at least wise to keep the waders on when fishing for salmon and trout. We even know of an expert fluke fisherman in New Jersey who never allows his hands to touch the cut bait. Perhaps he has something there.

Again for the benefit of those persons who are interested in anatomical matters—or in the "how" and the "why" of things—some brief notes. First of all, the outside of a fish's body is almost entirely covered by a layer of living skin that is protected by only a coating of slime. This is entirely unlike the human being, because, despite what some radio and television commercials would have us believe, our own skin is covered and protected by a layer of horny substance (*corneum*) that is "deader than the proverbial smelt."

In the second place, fish have glands at the surface of their bodies. They also possess certain specialized cells in their skin, called *chromatophores,* which have pigment and which can be expanded and contracted. And they have other cells that break up and refract light. Then, there is the silver or pearl essence in the skin of many fishes, which really is a waste product called *guanine* and which . . . but here we go getting technical again!

The sense of taste in fishes varies greatly with the species. Some fishes, for example, have "whiskers" or *barbels,* and these barbels have so-called *taste buds* at their tips, which enable the fish to detect food on the bottom without having to see or smell it. Catfish, carp, cod, and croakers are among the many bottom feeding species that have these special food detectors.

The significance of this type of mechanism to the angler is perhaps best exemplified by the catfish family and its well known member the lowly bullhead, or horned pout. And we know of no one who has described this relationship as exquisitely as an old friend, Albert Bromley, writing some years ago in the New York State *Conservationist:*

"As regards food, he is no epicure. Using his eight barbels, and probably his eyes to some extent, to read the menu along the bottom, he moves leisurely along engulfing nymphs and adult aquatic insects, freshwater mollusks, crustaceans and minnows of the slow cruising speed varieties. These he tops off with an aquatic salad of seeds and succulent greeneries from various sub-surface plants. This indiscriminating appetite gladdens the heart of the fisherman for, to quote Thoreau, 'They will take any kind of bait from an angleworm to a piece of tomato can and seldom fail to swallow the hook'.

"If you haven't already met this chap on the end of your fish line (and the chances are extremely remote that you haven't) there are a few pointers to be observed for a proper introduction. For your contemplated call select a warm spring night along in May. A fine drizzle with a gentle south breeze is prescribed. Shortly after dark be on your way equipped as follows: One bamboo pole (anything over ten feet preferred) with 30 to 50 feet of heavy line attached to the far end and wrapped spirally down the pole in such a manner as to place the hook in position to pierce your pants as you walk. For bait nightwalkers are prescribed with the No. 2 tomato can being the preferred carrier. Nevertheless there is a small group which leans to the Prince Albert tobacco can, several of which can be stowed on the person. This has disadvantages in the dark, however, if you are a pipe smoker. Other essentials are a kerosene lantern (the

smoky variety is the most common) and a jug of tea or
something for the marsh chill. A poll on the refreshment
problem among bullhead fishermen in upper New York
State showed hard cider to have a commanding lead.

"Thus prepared, proceed to a likely marsh, pond, or
river anywhere in the neighborhood. Having arrived (a
triumph in itself), deposit your gear, unroll your line,
get out your jackknife and cut the hook out of your
pants leg, attach a large cork bobber and a four to six-
ounce sinker. Such a sinker may outweigh any fish
caught but it's essential in securing a satisfactory splash
following a full swinging overhead cast. Bait up. No
need to hold the bamboo schooner mast, stick the butt
in the mud.

"You should soon have your first bite. Walk purpose-
fully to the pole and grasp firmly, right hand near the
butt and left as far out as possible. Place left foot in
front with knee bent. Now spring back, lifting mightily
at the same time and follow through with a complete
overhead maneuver. If this technique is fully mastered
your horned pout will be securely grounded some 50
feet to the rear where, with aid of lantern and matches
he can be located eventually.

"There's no hurry; time means nothing to bullheads."

BEHAVIOR

By all the professionally accepted standards that we
human beings measure intelligence, the fish is a very
stupid animal. In fact, the brain of a one-pound trout
would scarcely fill a fountain pen and even bears some
semblance to one. This does not mean that a fish cannot

detect our presence by sight, sound, or feel, or that it cannot possess or develop extreme wariness and quick responses or "learn" (become conditioned) through experience. It can. But the lowly nightwalker or dew worm, although deaf and "sightless" and with only a pair of tiny knobs or nerve ganglia serving as a poor excuse for a brain, also exhibits these characteristics to a marked degree—as those with aching backs who have hunted nightwalkers can quickly testify. In other words, the thing we correctly call *intelligence* has little if anything to do with those characteristics of fishes that can make them very difficult to catch on hook and line.

While this may seem beside the point and a mere matter of word quibbling, it is actually the most important difference between the angler, on the one hand, and his underwater quarry, on the other. For the angler has been gifted not only with the power of intuition, but also with the unique power of reason. This means that while the fish is unable to study and contemplate the angler, the angler is able to do this to the fish. Not only this, but he can also study, and reflect upon, the studies and reflections of other anglers—even of scientists. This gives—or should give—the angler a tremendous advantage over the fish, and the fact that it frequently does not is a matter that we have already dwelt upon, perhaps a bit too indelicately.

The actions and responses of fishes that so often baffle the angler and fool him into believing that fish are highly intelligent creatures, come about in three ways. First, as we have seen, fish are highly sensitive animals—even possessing a sort of sixth sense in their *lateral line*. Second, fish have many instincts or inherited

inner promptings to action. Finally, fish can "learn"
(become conditioned) from experience. This so-called
"learning" doesn't require any reasoning or big brain
power, and it may last for as little as a few minutes or
for more than several months; perhaps years. Some
species, e.g. the largemouth bass, can "learn" very
quickly, while others such as the northern pike and the
eastern chain pickerel can be very "fierce and stupid".
These are the characteristics of fishes—the key factors
shall we say—that are used by the fish to survive, but
which can be used by the angler to bring about its
downfall. Let us see how they may operate in practice.

Suppose we were to go fishing for largemouth bass
in some farm pond or small lake that had never been
fished before. Suppose we were to use underwater

artificials during the afternoon and surface lures at dusk, and *return every bass we caught to the water.* Would we catch bass easily, day after day as long as we kept throwing them back?

The answer, of course, is "No!" In fact our catches would probably start slowing down during a fast "opening" day, and continue to do so until it would be very difficult to catch a bass. In a farm pond of an acre or so things might become very difficult after about three days of fishing, while in a larger pond or small lake, it might require a week or longer. This is called "conditioning" from experience, but we'll just call it "learning"—however inaccurate the term may be—in order to simplify matters.

Field and laboratory experiments have shown that the *average* largemouth bass not only learns quickly, but can retain this learning for days, weeks, and perhaps years. One excellent example of this retention or "memory", was afforded a few years ago in our own experimental farm pond. Seventeen largemouths that had been trained in laboratory experiments not to take artificials, were stocked into the pond. For two summers afterward, not a bass was taken on artificials, despite a five-dollar reward for such a feat! This is not to say that none of the bass could have been taken on artificials, but it does indicate how quickly and thoroughly these fish had learned their lessons.

Other laboratory experiments on largemouth bass have shown that the species can quickly become "gut shy". In other words, after an experience or two, the average bass in these experiments would not take a live minnow that was attached to a hook and visible leader, but would strike at a free minnow. Even a 5X leader was apparently visible in clear water.

Sometimes it is difficult to know what a fish may have *inherited* and what it may have learned from experience. Bluefish, *Pomatomus saltatrix,* and common bonito, *Sarda sarda,* both seem to be *innately* "gut shy", and rainbow trout are not above suspicion. We have observed recently stocked rainbow trout veer away from a 4X leader with a No. 12 salmon egg hook buried in an oil pack, western salmon egg, only to feed quickly when a free egg was tossed in.

Mention of salmon eggs reminds us that trout—and particularly the rainbow trout—have a strong, *inherited* affinity for them. This is why salmon or trout eggs, when of the right type and when correctly used, are a very effective bait. In fact, this instinctive affinity for salmon or trout eggs can be used to evoke the *competitive urge* in trout by chumming with the eggs. Then, if some agitation of the water is present or added, three strong forces are at work simultaneously: competition, affinity for salmon or trout eggs, and the attraction of agitation. Needless to say, trout angling can be a massacre in such situations!

Not long ago we were discussing this matter of chumming trout in streams with a friend who is famous both as a dry fly purist and custom fly tier, but who knows all the tricks of the professional and has some genuine tolerance of "worm drowning," "amateurs delight" (spinning) and the other more plebian forms of angling. The discussion had reached a point where the folly of passing general laws against all use of salmon eggs had been agreed upon and the relative merits of salt water

grass shrimp, grasshoppers, and Japanese beetles as
chum were under meticulous consideration. We happened to observe that both grasshoppers and Japanese
beetles had a strong tendency to float in contrast to
salmon eggs and grass shrimp. Our friend, who is truly
one of the world's great creative artists in fly fishing,
remarked, quite simply:

"A good wetting agent sinks them perfectly. I once
chummed up all the trout in a big pool of the Beaverkill
with Japanese beetles!"

The affinity of most game fishes for agitated water is
something that has only recently become appreciated
by many fresh water anglers. Salt water anglers were
trolling for game fishes in the wash of a power boat for
years before fresh water anglers began to catch on.
We'll never forget the thrill of the discovery, in 1939,
that smallmouth bass, far from being frightened by a
slow or moderately speeded outboard, were actually
attracted by it and would strike lures trolled in the wash
of the outboard—sometimes when only ten feet from the
propeller—far more readily than when cast or when
trolled without agitation. Nor will we forget the thrill
received from testing this discovery in another lake
(Ontario) soon afterward. There were three of us
present on that occasion, and we had to sit in the stern
of the boat in order to slow it down. So we trolled our
weighted streamer flies in the big foaming wave about
30 feet behind the boat. And we caught bass after bass
while cruising among anglers who were quietly rowing
their boats and trolling crayfish, giving us some baleful
and incredulous looks.

During the past few years more and more of the angling fraternity seems to be stumbling upon the influence of competition and water agitation on fish behavior. This is seen in the trend toward the use of multiple or compound lures. Beginning with the sets of large flasher spoons trolled ahead of a bait (known as "cowbells" in some places) which were developed some years ago, there has been a growing tendency to troll two, or even three, streamer flies, and sometimes to use two plugs or other type of artificial—one behind the other—instead of the customary single lure. The development of the famous "Junk Lure" for striped bass on the Atlantic Coast during 1956 is another example of the trend. Chumming, of course, has been practiced extensively in salt water for many many years—perhaps centuries.

The competitive or "bullying" urges in game fishes can be very strong. This can be observed in the social hierarchies that fish promptly set up in aquaria or pools, and in their feeding behavior. Heavily gorged fish will often disgorge and continue to feed at the sight of a "competitor" chasing a bait fish.

The sudden flurries of feeding activity that fishes undergo from time to time is also an interesting phenomenon. Sometimes just a few fish at one location will go into one of these flurries. At other times large numbers of fish are involved over a wide area of fresh or salt water. These flurries may last for less than a minute or for several hours, and it is not definitely known just what causes or "triggers" them. They appear to be spontaneous reactions to some stimulus, just as huge rafts of ducks may appear to rise from the water all at

once. It is entirely possible, however, that some form
of communication or lightning-fast responses are involved.

It is always nice to be around at the exact spot and
time of these flurries. The fish are "eager beavers" and
far easier to catch than usual. But these orgies are rare
and unpredictable; and if we had to depend upon them
for catching fish, our creels and fish boxes would usually
be empty.

Some of the more popular theories—or, more accurately, hypotheses—about feeding activity in fishes
have been put to carefully designed, scientific tests,
but so far none of them has stood up to the tests. Indeed, one prominent fishery scientist discovered that
if enough of the various fishing calendars were consulted, almost every day of the year is a good fishing
day on some calendar! Similarly, certain hypotheses

concerning the position of the earth in relation to particular celestial bodies have failed to receive support when submitted to the objectivity of scientific tests.

On the other hand, temperature and temperature changes have been scientifically demonstrated again and again to be important influences on fish behavior. The influence can be direct, such as on the rate of digestion of food or on the preference of the fish, or it can be indirect such as through "learned" associations with food or other pleasant experiences. In fact, some fishes can detect temperature differences as small as one three-hundredths of a degree centigrade!

Fish have definite preferences for certain ranges of temperature. They also have certain ranges of temperature tolerance. Both the range of preference and the range of tolerance depend upon the species and, possibly, the strain of the species. The *preference range* can be loosely defined as that which the fish will not seek to leave under normal circumstances. The *tolerance range* represents the minimum and maximum temperatures that a fish can stand, more or less indefinitely, without passing out.

Usually, the food demand and rate of digestion have been found to increase as water temperature increases, until at or near the upper limit of temperature tolerance. On the other hand, some fishes, e.g. the lake trout or togue, exhibit a lower rate of metabolism with rise in water temperature, well below the upper limit of tolerance.

Strangely enough, these ranges of preference, together with temperature-food digestion rates, have been scientifically established for only a very few species. This does not mean that we don't know about temperature requirements and influences for many other species of fish. We do. But relatively few species have been put through laboratory paces for precise measurements. In later chapters we'll have much more to say, incidentally, about temperature and temperature changes as these affect fishes and their catchability.

There is abundant evidence to suggest that changes in atmospheric pressure (barometer) have an effect upon fish behavior and particularly feeding behavior, but scientific tests and measurements of the phenomena are again few and inconclusive. A rising barometer is usually associated with increased feeding activity, and a falling barometer with decreased activity. But we have been confounded on so many occasions by opposite behavior that, so far, we cannot go along with any conclusion in the matter.

One of the great difficulties in measuring the effect of a natural factor—e.g. the full moon or atmospheric pressure—upon the catchability of fish, is that other factors are so often tied up with the one we seek to measure. The full moon, for example, may mean calm cool weather with high pressure. If so, what is being tested? There is always something associated with a full moon or, for that matter, with no moon, or a half moon. It is only the incomplete angler out to convince himself, or the bogus authority out to convince many others, who goes for the "hocus pocus" stuff or who has the final answer about the moon and sun and gravity and pressure, etc., etc. The real pro looks to his lures, the species, the situation, and the presentation. And he knows, as the Good Book states, that "to him that

hath, more shall be given." He keeps his lamps well
oiled and leaves but little to luck and guesswork.

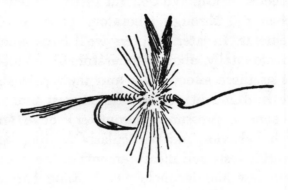

3

The Fish at Home —
In Lakes and Ponds

"Into this Universe, and Why not knowing
Nor Whence, like Water willy-nilly flowing
—Edward Fitzgerald

The home of all fishes is water in which there is an adequate supply of dissolved oxygen, some carbon dioxide, and a number of other impurities (chemical compounds) such as nitrates, phosphates, carbonates, sulfates, chlorides, etc. Natural sea water may have dozens of these ingredients—some in considerable quantity—while fresh water may have relatively few and all these in very minute quantities. Such a thing as absolutely pure water has probably never existed, and the so-called "chemically pure" water of the laboratory is far better suited for storage batteries, developing photographs, and washing clothes than for fish life. In fact, fish may die when they are placed in this "chemically pure" water—sometimes within a short time—even as they may die when placed in certain water that meets all standards for drinking.

It is the nature and amounts of these chemical ingredients or impurities in water which, together with temperature, depth, and water movement, largely determine what fishes will be present where and when. So let's examine these and other important aspects of the lake and pond homes of fishes and see how they affect both fish and fishing.

I.

When water becomes impounded, either by Nature or Man, some interesting things occur that are of great importance to fish and fishermen. In the first place, Nature seems to abhor the pond or lake that has been created—whether by Her or by Man—and seeks gradually to obliterate it with silt, with detritus from decaying vegetation, and by encroachment of plant life at the shores. These changes can be rapid or slow, depending upon the size of the impoundment and the particular situation. In the second place, the water doesn't just lie there as a uniform mass of liquid, but actually forms layers, or strata, of different temperatures. Unless the lake or pond is in the warmth of the deep South, these layers will form and re-form with the seasons, and their characteristics will have a profound effect upon fish life. In fact, this stratification largely determines what fish will be where and when. Finally, there is the matter of the chemical ingredients, or plant *nutrients* that may be present, and their consequent effect upon all life in the water, including fish.

If this sounds a bit complicated, it is actually a greatly oversimplified account of what goes on in a pond or lake and what is important to the distribution and behavior of fishes. For lakes and ponds are dynamic, constantly changing situations, and the study of their physical, chemical and biological characteristics constitutes the science known as *Limnology*. But again let's avoid becoming too technical, and rather attempt to reduce this complicated subject to practical fundamentals. Let's begin by describing the deep, "cool" lakes of the northern United States and Canada and then proceed to other types.

Probably the best examples of the deep, cool lakes of our Northeast are the Finger Lakes of New York State and the large, deep lakes of Ontario, Vermont, New Hampshire, and Maine. These lakes are usually what the limnologist calls *oligotrophic* lakes: They are characterized by a very large volume of water in relation to their surface area, and have large areas of sandy or rocky bottom. Extreme examples of this type of lake in our Northeast are found in some of the Finger Lakes of New York State. Some of these lakes e.g. Cayuga and Seneca—are more than 500 feet deep with bottoms below sea level. They are narrow, as their name implies, and their volumes are great in relation to their surface areas. Similarly, *oligotrophic* lakes in Ontario, New Hampshire or Maine—not to mention more western regions—may be more than 100 feet deep with only a few miles of surface area. Finally, these lakes are in our more northern latitudes and are exposed to winter temperatures that average well below freezing; the sun's rays strike them at a more oblique angle than farther south; and the quantity of dissolved plant nutrients in the water may be much less than in shallower lakes. All this means cooler, clearer water with more dissolved oxygen in the depths.

Now what do these deep, cool lakes look like at various times of year, and what is the effect of these seasonal characteristics upon fish? Let's start with a winter picture and follow through for an entire year.

If our lake is in Ontario, New Hampshire, Vermont, or Maine, its surface will be frozen over in the dead of winter by a foot or more of ice—possibly three feet.* The temperature of this ice may be 32° F. or many degrees below zero F., and it may rumble and crack as it tightens in the bitter cold of winter. But the water in the depths will probably be 39.2° F., because water is at its densest, or heaviest, at this temperature and sinks to the bottom.

Here we may receive our first surprise: for, the ice fisherman catching yellow perch as far south as New Jersey, the whitefish fisherman in Ontario, the smelt fisherman in Maine or New Brunswick, and the northern pike and walleye fisherman in New York or Wisconsin —all these ice anglers may be catching their fish from water of the same temperature!

When "ice out" occurs in spring or early summer, a profound change takes place in these lakes. As the surface water warms and reaches the temperature of the depths, convection currents are present throughout the lake, and the water, in a sense, becomes homogenized. This is the time that many anglers have looked forward to and prepared for all winter, because this is the time when lake trout, landlocked salmon, rainbows and squaretails can be taken close to the shore and at

---

* The larger Finger Lakes, like the Great Lakes, have great volumes of water—particularly in relation to their surface—and do not freeze over except under most unusual circumstances.

the surface. A card, a telegram, a phone call, and these anglers begin packing their automobiles—perhaps a thousand miles away!

With the onset of summer another great change begins to take place in these lakes: The rays of the sun continue to warm the water—slowly but surely—and the water responds by forming layers, or strata, of different temperatures. A warm surface layer forms, with a second layer directly beneath it of rapidly descending temperatures. Beneath this, and all the way to the bottom, is a cold layer. (Limnologists have special names for these layers as can be seen from our illustration). At the beginning of the summer the upper, warm layer, or *epilimnion* may be only a few inches deep, but by late summer it may be upwards of 30 feet deep! The layer of rapidly descending temperatures, or *thermocline*, directly beneath may be four to 20 feet deep and the remainder, or *hypolimnion*, will have little change in temperature all the way to the bottom. The temperatures in the depths? If the lake is more than 70 feet deep, the chances are that the temperature at the bottom will be—you guessed it—39.2° F., or not much higher!

Now, this division of the lake into three layers, or

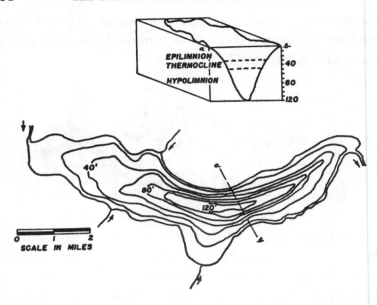

strata, of different temperatures will obviously have an effect upon the distribution of the fishes in the lake. The lake trout or togue, for example, will move into the cold depths and will be joined by whitefish, smelt, deep water sculpins, deep water sticklebacks, ciscos, ling—or whatever of these species happens to be present in the lake—because these are the species that prefer these cold temperatures. Landlocked salmon, alewife herring or "sawbellies", some of the smelts and ciscos, rainbow, brook and brown trout will usually prefer the temperatures in or just below the thermocline—that intermediate layer of rapidly decreasing temperature directly beneath the warm water or *epilimnion.*

This condition of stratification—which in a sense is three separate lakes one above the other—persists until late summer or fall or until the surface temperature descends to that of the depths. At this time convection

currents again run wild and the lake "turns over" and
again becomes "homogenized". And in like manner the
species mingle with one another: the lake trout, the
bass, the ciscos, the landlocked salmon, the perch, the
browns, brooks, rainbows—whatever is present. Then
winter sets in with the ice conditions we have already
described and the completion of the cycle.

So far we have described only the general effects
upon fishes of the seasonal behavior of this type of lake.
But what of the specific effects upon particular species
and how do these affect our angling success? Here we
must divide our lakes into geographic regions—more
eastern or more western—and upon the additional basis
of their past stocking and management. And we must
also remember that no two lakes are *exactly* the same
no matter how near to each other they may be situated
or how close their ages may be. Perhaps our best approach would be to consider a particular lake that may
be representative of many other lakes insofar as our
angling efforts are concerned. Let's begin with an
oligotrophic lake in Maine that supports landlocked
salmon, smallmouth bass, whitefish, smelt, and lake
trout—or togue as they are called by our downeaster
friends.

At ice-out—that rather sudden and dramatic event
of spring which usually seems to be overdue—the sun
may be hot and the nights freezing cold. Or it may be
just bleak and cold, period! But the tree buds will be
swelling and beginning to burst, and the chirp of a
robin or the flash of a warbler in the trees is comforting
reassurance that you have judged things correctly. The
lake water is "ice cold"—which may mean anything

from 37° F. to 50° F. But unless you are curious about such things you won't worry about it. (P.S. It will probably be about 40° F.)

It is at this time that the water in the lake is "homogenized" after its winter of stratification, and it is at this time that the various fishes in the lake are wandering all over the place—lake trout, landlocked salmon, smelt, smallmouth bass, and all the rest. It is a sort of upheaval time for water and fish, despite the fact that smallmouth bass are not yet ready to feed actively and despite the fact that smelt have something other than food on their mind (We are referring, of course, to sex).

This is also an upheaval time in the soul of the angler who knows about these things and who has planned his trip all winter. Because this is the time that the landlocked salmon and the lake trout can be found close to shore and ready to take a well presented streamer fly or piece of metal. The nightly romances of the smelt under a full moon accompanied by an orchestra of spring peepers and other songs of the night are also known to him, and he can feel like Isaak Walton did some 300 years before:

> *"Here, give my weary spirits rest*
> *And raise my low-pitched thoughts above*
> *Earth, or what poor mortals love.*
> *Thus, free from lawsuits, and the noise*
> *of princes' courts, I would rejoice;"*

The spawning runs of smelt into the streams, brooks, and freshets at this time of year provide one of the great spectacles of nature. In some lakes the adult smelt are

tiny and needle-like from poor growing conditions, and
are difficult to observe. But in other lakes they reach a
size of six inches or larger—the smelt of commerce—
and can be easily seen under the beam of a flashlight or
even under the light of a full moon.

In daytime the smelt remain in the general vicinity of
the brook or freshet that they will later ascend under
the cover of darkness. Shortly after sundown they begin
to congregate at the entrance of the stream, and by
nightfall the "run is on" as they push their way up
through the shallow, running water. If the run is a large
one, the first few hundred feet of the brooklet can soon
become swollen with smelt, with other hordes waiting
around the entrance for a chance to enter. So crowded
can they become that it is a simple matter to reach
down and pick them up with your bare hands.

Needless to say, laws have been passed by Maine and
other states where smelt occur, to protect the species
during this time of complete vulnerability. Yet, the
temptation to pocket a few of these delectable morsels
for the frying pan is sometimes overwhelming, as an
old and close friend learned recently to his great embarrassment. It was during a salmon safari with three companions to one of Maine's finest lakes, and we report
his account here not only because of its vivid description of a smelt run, but also because of the human
conflict of values in which our friend found himself.
Again, names have been changed or omitted to protect
both the innocent and the guilty:

*"It was one of those perfect nights, when the sun
had set clear and the spring peepers had strung up early*

and were in full rhythm. Every once in a while you could hear the sustained, mellow note of a common toad behind the chorus of peepers.

"We parked the car on a dirt road where a little brook went through a culvert about a quarter mile above the lake. We then walked down a tote road that was half full of logs and which ran parallel to the stream about a hundred feet away. I was glad that I had worn my woolen hunting coat, because the temperature was close to freezing. I remember buttoning the coat as I walked down the tote road.

"The road opened onto a small sand beach, and there was the big lake, somewhat vague under the moonlight but with a surface that was as still as molten metal! It was one of those dreambook scenes and you paused for a minute to take it all in. As we walked toward the entrance of the stream it was obvious that the smelt were in, because you could both hear and see them shower the surface along the shore as they took alarm.

"Arriving at the mouth of the brook, we walked up about 30 feet to where it was narrow and the water flowing, and turned on our flashlight. The little stream was packed solid and black with smelt! You couldn't see the bottom. They just lay there, undulating slightly with the current, layer upon layer and pushing each other out onto the banks! I reached down and picked up three or four of them in my hand and noticed that all but one had rough scales. Obviously these rough ones were males. But it was early in the evening and the males were first as usual.

"I turned off my flashlight and began to walk upstream, oblivious of my companions and flashing my

*light from time to time into the brook. The scene was
the same: smelt and more smelt. I became curious at
this time about the number of eggs that this great mass
of fish might be laying, so I began to examine the stones
and gravel on the bottom of the stream. They were
covered by a solid mass of jelly—the adhesive eggs of
the smelt—and the eggs were already layer upon layer
at this early hour of the run. No wonder some of the
biologists are thinking about broadening these brooks
to increase the smelt population. Many of these eggs
must smother themselves by their sheer mass!*

*"Anyway, I walked upstream a little farther and
noticed that the water was running faster and that
there were fewer smelt. As you know, they can't take
the very fast water. So I walked to the car and waited
for my three companions. They were along in a
moment."*

At this point in his account our friend seemed to
become a bit concerned. He began to frown slightly
and went out to the kitchen to pour himself another
drink. When he came back, he didn't sit down but
paced the room slowly, holding his drink in his hand
and looking towards the floor. He continued his story:

*"You know, I lean over backwards to observe the
letter of the law in fish and game matters. Not that
I've always been that way—in fact I used to get a thrill
out of poaching and took great satisfaction in being
good at it! But middle age does something to a person—
or at least it should. You begin to realize that there's
much more to life than the old rat race, and this dis-*

covery opens new horizons for you: you can really relax and explore, for a change, and not worry about constantly proving your prowess.

"It never occurred to me to sneak smelt out of this stream, nor did it occur to me that my companions might be so tempted. In fact, it was not until we were in the car and about halfway back to the cabins that the smell of smelt made me suspect the worst. You know that unique, metallic odor of the smelt. There's nothing else like it!

"Sure enough when we arrived at the camp, my companions began whooping it up and pulling smelt out of the pockets of their hunting coats. They piled the silvery morsels on a plate in front of me and waited for my reaction.

"What did I do?

"Hell, I just asked if we had enough butter."

Smelt in some lakes may spawn on bars, shoals, or in coves. But regardless of the actual place, the behavior of these little fish is of great importance to the togue and landlocked salmon fishermen. For both salmon and togue feed heavily upon smelt and have a strong tendency to lurk near the smelt's spawning grounds at this time of year. Areas near the mouths of streams and freshets, the margins of ledges—or even on the ledges themselves to within a few feet of land—any or all of these may be productive.

The entrances of "smelt run" brooklets are often difficult to locate from a boat, and here we can sometimes receive an assist from our mischievous black friend the crow. Crows, like many humans, are very fond of fresh smelt, but have the advantage of aerial reconnaissance in locating smelt runs. Keep an eye on these crows, and when you see one emerge from the woods with a silvery object in its bill, mark down the spot. Chances are you will find a hidden brooklet that was the scene of much spawning activity the night before!

With the passing of the days and weeks after ice-out, and with the formation and gradual thickening of the warm surface layer, gradual changes take place in the behavior of the fishes. The lake trout or togue, which prefers the cold cold water, begins to disappear from the shore or *littoral* zone along with the smelt. If whitefish have been seeking food in the shallows, they too join the offshore movement. Meanwhile, the warming and thickening upper layer of water—the *epilimnion*—is re-

viving the smallmouth bass from its winter lethargy,
and this superb game fish begins to go on the prowl.

And the Silver King or landlocked salmon?

Fortunately, this species is less affected by temperature and, like the squaretail, often continues to play
the shoreline for many weeks. Indeed, it will often break
through the *thermocline* into the warm *epilimnion—*
sometimes until midsummer—and is seldom out of the
range of moderately light tackle. (We will have more
to say about this in the chapters on angling methods).

At this point in our account, an astute reader may
ask, "Is it possible to catch both landlocked salmon and
smallmouth bass at the same time of year? The answer,
of course, is "Yes, if you hit conditions at just the right
time." In fact we have occasionally caught landlocked
salmon, togue, and smallmouth bass all in the same day
on a Maine lake without changing lures and at a time
and circumstance when all three species were legal to
retain. And there are areas in Maine e.g. the St. Croix
River drainage—where excellent salmon lakes are only
short distances from superb smallmouth resources. During the first three weeks of June, for example, the angler
who loves both species can get into a real quandary over
just what lake to fish on a particular day!

When the temperature of the *epilimnion* in our Maine
lake reaches 60° F., its thickness may be ten feet or
more, and the smallmouth bass begins to be stimulated
by the reproductive urge. Male smallmouths commence
nest building and will soon be poised over the depressions they have formed in the bottom. These nests may
be in two feet of water or, perhaps, 12 feet.

The hatching of the eggs in the nest requires only a

few days, and unlike its relative the largemouth bass, *M. dolomieu* will pay no attention to the young after they begin to swim around. For a time—perhaps two to four weeks—the smallmouths, both male and female, will lurk in the shallow water before moving to the edges of shoals and shore shelves for bottom feeding. This usually takes place in late June or early July in our more northern latitudes.

From midsummer to the crisp days of autumn, the landlocked salmon, the smallmouth bass and the lake trout are in special places in their home and require special—and often not very satisfying—techniques to catch them. This fact has often seemed to us as a bit unjust to the North American angler who so often takes his vacation during the month of August. For not only are the game fishes of our Maine lake more uncooperative at this time of year, but so also are the game fishes of most lakes!

By midsummer, then, we have located the landlocked salmon in or below the *thermocline,* the smallmouth bass fairly deep on the margins of the ledges, and the togue and whitefish away down near or on the bottom in upwards of 60 feet of water. Of the four species, the smallmouth is the most cooperative to the light tackle enthusiast at this time of year, because the species has the habit of feeding in the shallows after sundown, before sunup, and during heavy overcasts.

With the onset of autumn and its quiet air, late summer haze, reduced angle of sun, and glow of late harvest, the fishes of our Maine lake are again stimulated to change their ways. The smallmouth bass may begin to cruise the shallows again during the day, and move about much more widely in search of food. The lake trout and the landlocked salmon have ripening gonads, and sex hormones are beginning to course through their bodies. These fish, too, gradually move to the shallower areas.

Meanwhile, the surface waters are cooling and soon the lake goes into its homogenizing process. The togue usually seek gravel or stony bars on which to spawn, and the landlocked salmon seek the inlets or outlets of the lake to build their nests, or *redds*, in flowing water. Whitefish also seek shallower areas and broadcast their eggs over the bottom. Finally, ice begins to creep over the surface of the lake and soon all is sealed over for the winter. Only the cold cold water species—the lake trout, the whitefish, the little smelt and the landlocked salmon—actively go about in search of food. Even the squaretail, or speckled trout, is a bit lethargic at 40° F.

Not all of the deep, cool lakes of Maine have the same species of fish in them as the one we have just described. Some do not have any landlocked salmon; others with salmon may not have any bass or, perhaps, togue; while still others may have all these plus white perch, pickerel, and a whole host of forage fishes. As we have stated, no two lakes are exactly the same, and this is true whether we consider them physically, chemically, or biologically.

III.

When we turn our attention to the deep, cool lakes of the Great Lakes drainage system (we are not yet ready to consider "warm", shallow lakes), much that we have learned about our Maine lake can be of value to us when we fish any oligotrophic lake of this vast area. The seasonal behavior of the water will be the same; the behavior of the species we have encountered will be generally the same; and again there will be much rock and sand on the bottom. We will, however, almost have to bid farewell to some good old piscatorial friends, again greet some familiar faces, and be prepared to meet some important new ones.

Absent, for example (except upon rare occasion), will be the landlocked salmon, the eastern chain pickerel, and the white perch. Usually present will be the togue (now called lake trout or salmon trout), the squaretail (now called brook trout, speckled trout, or native trout), and the smallmouth bass. Among the "strangers" will be the abundant cisco—a coldwater cousin of the white-fish—the delicious walleyed pike or, more correctly, pike-perch (called pickerel in Ontario), the great northern pike, and occasionally, that fabulous monster demon of fresh water, the muskellunge.* Let us meet these new-comers and see how they live in ponds and lakes.

We have already met the cisco—though briefly—in person. It is one of those fishes with the suspiciously large eye. Remember? Ciscos—sometimes called herring, bluebacks, greenbacks, etc.—look like the famous white-fish except that they have terminal rather than inferior mouths. This terminal mouth may not have come about by accident, because it is in keeping with the cisco's

---

* Walleyes, great northern pike, and muskellunge are usually associated with "warm" waters and weedy areas. Many lakes of the Great Lakes system, however, are vast and combine deep, cold water with large, shallow bays.

habit of feeding upon microscopic animal organisms that are suspended in the water, rather than upon bottom organisms. Ciscos are nearly always far more abundant than whitefish wherever the two species occur, and, as we have mentioned, can often be taken on hook and line by anglers who have the "know-how".

Our chief reason for formally introducing the cisco is the fact that in most of the oligotrophic lakes of the Great Lakes drainage system, the cisco—rather than the smelt—is the chief food of the lake trout. And this is probably why record breaking lake trout come from this area. In the lakes of the Atlantic coast drainages, for example, we hear of state record lake trout of 26 or perhaps 28 pounds. But these are small in comparison to the many lake trout of 30 to 40 pounds taken in some Ontario lakes, and are veritable "pee-wees" when compared to the great "siscowets" of Lake Superior, which have reportedly weighed in at over 70 pounds!

Yellow perch seem to be far more important as a panfish and as a forage item for game fish in the Great Lakes drainage than in Atlantic coastal drainages. Yellow perch have a wide range of temperature tolerance, feed actively at near freezing temperatures, and seem to be just as at home in 60 feet of water as in six.

The so-called "walleyed pike" which, as we have mentioned, is known as pickerel in Ontario, is neither a pike nor a pickerel, but actually another member of the perch family. And like the yellow perch, it is a schooling fish that feeds actively at very low water temperatures, is superb eating, and occurs in both shallow and fairly deep water. Unlike the yellow perch, however, which lays its gelatinous covered eggs in still waters, the walleye deposits its adhesive eggs on gravel or rubble bottom in moving water. Walleyes are present in some of the smaller oligotrophic lakes, but usually only when such lakes are part of a river chain or have been stocked.

The great northern pike in the Great Lakes drainage system—also a "warmwater" species—is a larger counterpart of the eastern chain pickerel of Atlantic coastal drainages. Despite its much greater size, however, the northern pike is not the inch-for-inch fighter that the chain pickerel is. In fact, the latter more closely resembles the muskellunge in both fighting spirit and tactics. Pike, nevertheless, are a fine game fish after they have reached five or six pounds in weight—a size that is very large for a pickerel.

The muskellunge is the largest member of the pike family, and seems to require "big water" and much territory in order to spawn and survive naturally. They are a solitary type of fish, and with their rather extensive territorial demand, are seldom, if ever, as abundant as great northern pike.

The largemouth bass often occurs in deep "cold" lakes that have shallow, weedy coves. In areas of water lilies, for instance, the largemouths tend to lurk near "openings" in the lily pads or along the outer margins of the beds.

Now, how do these "newcomers"—the cisco, the great northern pike, the muskellunge, the yellow perch and the "walleye"—respond to the seasonal changes in the lake, and where do they live at different times of year?

With the ice-out in spring and the "homogenization" of the water, the cisco, along with the whitefish, may be distributed rather extensively—in shallow water as well as deep water.

The northern pike lurks in the lagoons and certain other shallow areas of the lake. Pike will soon spawn in these areas—usually at daybreak—and their eggs will sink to the bottom or into the vegetation. The newly hatched pike larvae will remain on the bottom or be stuck to the vegetation for several days by means of an adhesive organ on the tops of their heads.

Muskellunge, when present, also spawn at this time of year and in the manner of the great northern pike.

Walleyed pike, on the other hand, will seek out their spawning rivers or shoals and gather *en masse*—usually at night. Their eggs stick to the gravel or rubble on the bottom, and the species is usually protected at this time.

Yellow perch congregate in certain coves and lagoons, and their eggs appear as gelatinous masses on the bottom, or attached to submerged brush somewhat in the manner of frogs' eggs.

As the surface and shallow waters become much warmer—say about 60° F.—the walleyes, pike, and muskellunge will seek deeper regions, but seldom more than 40 feet. In other words they will tend to remain in the "warm" water. All these fishes moreover—and particularly pike and muskellunge—will tend to lurk in or near weed beds.

Walleyes, as we have mentioned, are a schooling fish, and when a feeding school is located, they can often be taken one after another—particularly during overcast days or after sundown.

Yellow perch, also a schooling species, tend to remain

in shallow water during the early weeks of summer. They then tend to move into deeper water and beds of submerged vegetation.

Now what will one of these composite, or combination, types of lakes look like in midsummer and how will the fishes be distributed?

Admittedly, there are relatively few of these composite lakes—large lakes that combine "cold" deepwater regions with extensive shallow areas of "warm" water. Yet there are a number of them in the Great Lakes drainage, including the Great Lakes themselves. So let's take a careful look at the following illustrations.

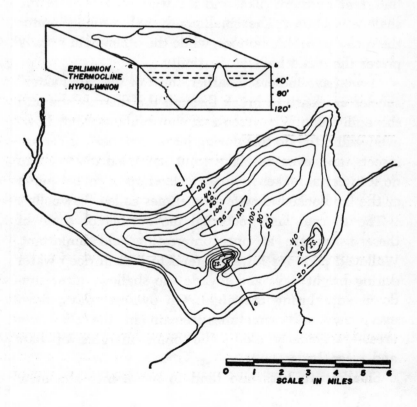

Note here that there are extensive shallow areas adjacent to a deep section. Also note that the upper, "warm" stratum—the epilimnion in the profile diagram —is continuous with the shallow areas. In other words the shallow areas are only slightly stratified.

By midsummer, the "coldwater" species, e.g. lake trout, rainbow trout, whitefish, cisco—will be in the deep .section of the lake: The lake trout, cisco, and whitefish will be at or near the bottom, and the rainbow trout probably in, or just below, the thermocline. The "warmwater" species, e.g. the smallmouth and largemouth bass and other sunfishes, the yellow perch, the great northern pike, and the walleye will be in the shallow sections. The smallmouth will usually prefer the rocky or rubble bottom, while the others will usually prefer the weed beds or proximity.

As we have indicated earlier, most of the "coldwater" species are loath to break through the thermocline into the epilimnion. The cisco and the rainbow trout, however, will often do this during large "hatches" of certain insects, and even the lake trout has been observed to do it in certain lakes in order to feed upon yellow perch or the landlocked alewife—sometimes called "sawbelly".

The diurnal and nocturnal movements of some of these fishes are at once interesting and important. Walleyed pike, for instance, tend to lurk in deep water during bright days and invade the shallows after sundown and during the night. On overcast days, however, they will sometimes remain in the shallower areas—particularly along the outer margins of bars and weed beds.

Smallmouth bass also tend to move into shallower

water for feeding after sundown but will sometimes "sun" themselves on shallow ledges on bright calm days. Often, yellow perch of various sizes will be mixed with the bass during these occasions, and apparently no effort is made by the bass to feed upon the perch during these siestas! Smallmouth bass are chiefly bottom feeders, after midsummer, in lakes that have an abundance of crayfish and other bottom organisms.

The largemouth bass, like the muskellunge, is one of the most unpredictable of fishes. Sometimes largemouths will cruise singly, or in pairs, for feeding during bright sunlight; at other times they will sulk during the day and feed actively at night; while on still other occasions they will congregate on a bar and feed actively during late evening. But here we are discussing "warmwater" fishes and situations, and it's time to consider the shallow types of lakes and ponds.

III.

Probably the best way to illustrate a shallow, "warmwater" lake is to take the last lake we considered and reduce the scale of depth contours and miles. It appears below.

Now some persons might consider this a pond, and other persons might consider a much smaller body of water to be a lake! But it makes little difference for the purpose at hand.

One of the most interesting and important phenomena of "shallow" lakes is the behavior of the water. Many such lakes—and particularly those north of ap-

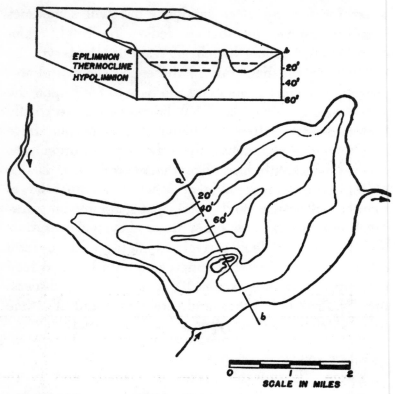

proximately 41° N. latitude—may have poorly defined stratification during the summer months. In fact, some of them may not stratify at all. On the other hand, other "shallow" lakes may not only stratify, but also have a depletion of dissolved oxygen in the *hypolimnium* at this time. The following illustration of a New Jersey pond shows this phenomenon.

Fishes, of course, cannot live for long in water that is deficient in dissolved oxygen. The deeper, cool water of a lake or pond, therefore, may be devoid of fish life during summer.

Shallow lakes and ponds usually have large areas of

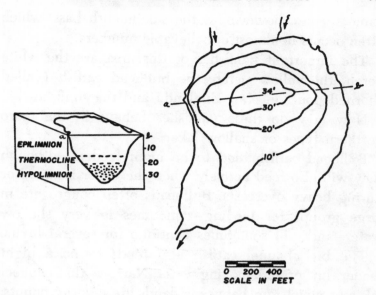

muck bottoms and weeds. In fact this muck bottom often accounts for "bottomless" lakes: the muck is so soft that it is sometimes almost impossible to determine when a small weight has reached the bottom.

Large, "warmwater" lakes in Canada and in the northern part of United States furnish some of the best freshwater angling on the North American continent. In the Great Lakes and St. Lawrence River drainages, there are muskellunge, great northern pike, smallmouth bass, largemouth bass, and walleyed pike as "warmwater" game species. Then, of course, there are the so-called "panfishes" such as yellow perch, bluegill and common sunfish, crappie, white or silver bass, bullhead catfish and the large, channel or lake catfish.

In the shallow lakes of the North Atlantic coastal drainages, there are eastern chain pickerel, smallmouth bass, and largemouth bass. The chief "warmwater" game species, however, is the smallmouth bass, which often occurs in almost unbelievable numbers.

The important panfishes of this area are the white perch, the yellow perch, the bullhead catfish (called "horned pout" in New England) and the sunfishes.

Now how do these panfishes behave in the more northern types of shallow lake?

Bullhead catfish tend to be night feeders, although they will also feed actively when the water is roiled or during heavy overcasts. Bullheads often congregate in large groups for feeding—sometimes in very shallow water—and will sometimes continue for several hours.

The big channel catfish also tends to be a night feeder, but prefers moving water. Narrows that connect lakes or which run between islands are favorite haunts, at depths up to 30 feet or so.

White perch and white or silver bass are—unlike smallmouths and largemouths—members of the bass family. (The so-called largemouth and smallmouth bass are members of the sunfish family.) White perch inhabit many lakes—both the "coldwater" and "warmwater" types—of the Atlantic coastal drainages, and are just as at home in the brackish water of river estuaries as in fresh water. They are a school fish and tend to congregate in certain areas of a lake.

White or silver bass are also a school fish, but are far less common than white perch and do not naturally inhabit waters of the Atlantic coastal drainages.

All of these panfishes are strongly influenced by water temperatures and seldom provide good ice fishing. The spawning habits of the bluegill, the pumpkinseed, and the crappies (called "calicos" in some areas), however, create excellent conditions for fly fishing: all of them, for instance, are nest builders in shallow to moderately shallow water. This takes place during spring or early summer, and the males zealously guard the nests and eggs. It is usually a simple matter to locate these nesting sites and capture a creel full of these delicious "pansters."

Ponds and lakes in the central and southern regions of United States frequently offer a different type of fishing situation: The waters are usually well stratified during the summer months, and very often there is little— if any—dissolved oxygen in the *hypolimnium*. The waters of the *epilimnion* are usually somewhat turbid from the bloom of microscopic plant life, and often have a brownish green cast from this bloom.

Such lakes are nearly always "saturated" with fish life, but usually with the "pan" or "weed" species. In other words, sunfish, golden shiners, suckers, and other "nongame" species are so abundant that, like weeds in a garden, they tend to hold down the number of largemouth bass, pickerel, or other game species.

This "imbalance" of weed to game species is the factor that is chiefly responsible for the "fishing doldrums" of such lakes and ponds during summer. It has the opposite effect upon the sunfishes, however, because the crowding creates sharp competition for food. Sunfish— bluegill, common etc.—not only are nest predators of the largemouth bass, but also compete for space in the water and for foods that are consumed by young game fishes. This tends to hold down the number of these game fish. Then, after the panfishes and golden shiners etc. have spawned—usually by midsummer—there is a great surplus of food for the game species. It is difficult to exaggerate the abundance of these weed species. In many lakes, for example, it has been found that eastern chain pickerel will feed almost entirely upon sunfish even though golden shiners may be even more abundant. The sunfish, it would appear, are easier to catch!

Fishery scientists have discovered that many lakes and ponds can be renovated from such a condition. This "home renovation" consists of poisoning all the fish in a lake by the use of rotenone—an insecticide that is not poisonous to warm-blooded animals. The lake is then stocked with the most suitable combination of fishes.

The maps of the homes of lake and pond fishes—such as the maps we have just considered—are one of the most valuable items of angling equipment. This is particularly true when an unfamiliar lake or pond is to be fished. A number of states and some of the Canadian provinces have surveyed many, if not all, of their lakes, and have published these maps. Some have been done in great detail, with such features as types of bottom, shoreline, and vegetation clearly indicated. Consulting or obtaining these maps can be a most worthwhile investment!

IV.

No chapter on lakes and ponds would be complete without some special reference to the so-called "farm pond." We say "so-called" because now a great many of these ponds are estate ponds or just home ponds. The population shift to the suburbs and the purchasing of small acreage has popularized the small pond just as it has the swimming pool. Largemouth bass and blue-gill are the usual fish combination, although large-mouths with golden shiners are often preferred north of the Mason-Dixon line where growing conditions are slower.

What can be gained from a small pond? Perhaps we should just quote from an outdoor column we wrote on this subject and which appeared in the Plainfield, N. J. *Courier-News:*

"It doesn't have to be a large pond. A small one will do—say an eighth acre or so—and if built near the house it's certainly nice to lie in bed on a hot summer night and hear the splash of a big bass out there in the darkness.

"It's also nice when you get up in the morning and look out and see the quiet surface of the pond in the early morning sunlight. The kids will probably be fishing before nightfall, and it will be refreshing to take a swim in the afternoon when the air temperature will be about 90!

"Then, of course, there was that late autumn dawn last year when the rising mist almost hid the pond and those four foolish mallards set in. Was it luck that you just happened to have the old 12 gauge handy and got two of them on the rise?

"A million dollar estate? No—just an abandoned farm with a big old house (in bad repair) which cost less

than a small residence in a development. Work? Yes—
plenty of it for a few years, but fun if you like it.

"There are many other advantages in a small pond.
If the property is not situated on a fire hydrant line,
for instance, a small pond can drastically reduce fire
insurance premiums. And the pond can also add more
equity to the property than the cost of its construction.

"Bait minnows, such as golden shiners, can usually be
produced by the thousands in an eighth acre pond each
year, and the retail price may be as high as 60 cents per
dozen.

"The cost of building a small pond varies greatly with
the situation. If bedrock—even soft shale—is present, the
cost may exceed $1,500. If, on the other hand, a bull-
dozer can do the job quickly, the cost may be less than
$500. A lowland area with good seepage, or a spot ad-
jacent to a small stream, are both usually well suited
for a pond site.

"For reduced insurance rates when away from a fire
hydrant line, certain requirements must be met. The
pond must contain a minimum of 100,000 gallons of
water at all times, and a stone or other hard top roadway
must extend to within ten feet of a spot in the pond that
has a minimum of three feet of water (four feet is preferred). The pond must also be within 600 feet of the
insured buildings.

"Then there are the frozen assets. There is the winter,
for instance, when the bitter cold nights form a thick
layer of blue-gray ice on the pond and the wind driven
snow flecks its surface. This is the time when the steel
blades of ice skates rumble and scrape in an accompani-
ment to the sounds of children's voices. And this is the

time when the bass are lethargic, but heavy with eggs and sperm in the waters beneath the ice. Indeed, this is the time when all of Nature seems to be resting, yet preparing its investment for the future.

"The small pond is well worth the cost."

4

The Fish at Home
In Streams and Rivers

*"The pleasant'st angling is to see the fish
Cut with her golden oars the silvery stream
And greedily devour the treacherous bait . . .*
—Shakespeare

M an has been deeply attracted by streams and rivers
since his origin upon Earth; and an angler who fishes
running water may soon forsake all other types of
angling in order to pursue this one form of the sport.
This is particularly true of trout fishermen, who find in
the boiling riffles, the glistening runs and the deep pools,
a contemplative retreat that becomes a veritable kingdom of heaven.

Needless to say, this total involvement does not begin
or end at the water's edge. It continues to haunt the
stricken angler to the extent that he lines his den with
stuffed fish, books on trout fishing and entomology,
rods, photographs and other paraphernalia. His desk is
seldom without a fly tying vise where his papers should
be, and the remainder is piled high with colorful
mounds of feathers, bucktail, Impala and Mongo tails,
thread, beeswax, clothespins, tweezers, a special lamp

etc. There may even be some empty beer bottles under-
neath it all. For of such is the kingdom of heaven to
this type of fisherman.

Is it small wonder, then, that the "little woman" may
(1) shrug her shoulders and resign, or (2) "blow her
stack" well before the Ides of March?

Or perhaps the L.W. loves to fish herself, feels the
challenge of it all, and wants to be helpful. In this case
she is apt to sneak into the den during her hero's absence, examine his progress and take mental note of
his errors. Her Woman's Intuition—note the capital let-
ters—tells her at once that Joe has erred by using yellow
chenille for the body of that streamer when obviously
any red-blooded fish would go for peacock herl. Of
course she doesn't tell this to Joe. She simply fails to
share his enthusiasm for his super-duper creation when
he announces it, and this is enough. An inevitable con-
versation ensues.

"You don't like it, do you?"

"Oh yes. I like it. In fact I think it's swell."

"But obviously there's something wrong with it, isn't
there?"

"I didn't say that."

"But that's what you're thinking. Now what's wrong
with it?"

"I didn't say there's anything wrong with it. That's
what you said."

"O.K., Genius. Let's see you create and tie up a big
deal."

"Now see here, Boy. You're the professed genius.
You know I don't tie flies. But if you don't know enough
to make that body out of peacock herl instead of that

stuff you're using, you should have your head examined."

This, of course, is the information that Joe has been seeking. He has been married to his favorite fishing companion for many years and has learned that the big music of happy marriage is contrapuntal as well as harmonic. And he has also learned that "Woman's Intuition" may be rewardingly correct. So he makes a second streamer with peacock herl and contemplates the future testing with pleasure and determination.

Not all of man's devotion and dedication to stream and river fishing is limited to trout anglers. There are other charms—even to the most "lowly". In the spring of the year, for instance, many streams are invaded by the bony, common sucker, and the pursuit of these fish at night with spear and lantern can also be a form of contemplative fishing at its highest:

"April is the month, generally, and the country boy knows just when. There's a half-warmth, a special texture to the spring night air. This is the night the run begins! So with gas lantern and boots, gunny sack and spear, you are on the stream—to look for swift shadows of elusive, running fish; to hear the spring peepers in the flooded grasslands, to feel the press of water against your legs. And there is the smell of thawing earth; of the fresh surging stream and of fish." *

But let's get back to the fish at home.

River drainages—or watersheds—usually bear a great resemblance to one another. On a map they resemble a tree with many twigs, branches and limbs, and with a trunk that may be very wide at the bottom. Some river systems may be very small—such as many along our coasts. Others may drain several states while one, the Amazon, may drain the major area of a huge continent.

For practical purposes, let us consider a river system that is moderately large, which offers a variety of angling for millions of people from its origin to the sea, and which is destined for much future "development" in the form of reservoir construction.

The illustration below is of the Delaware—a river that has its origin in a myriad of cold trickles and seepages of the gray sandstones deep in the Catskills of New York State. These origins soon become brooks and streams that form two main branches—the West Branch and the East Branch of the Delaware. Contributing to the flow of the East Branch are two famous brown trout streams, the Beaverkill and the Willowemoc, which join together some miles above the junction of the former with the Delaware. The course of the Delaware on its journey

---

* Albert Bromley in the N. Y. CONSERVATIONIST.

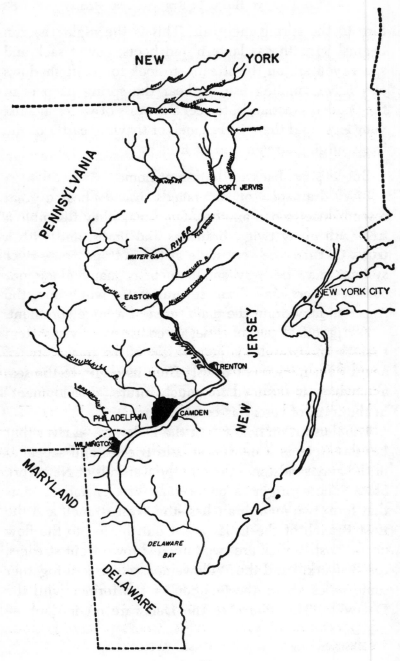

to the sea then involves four states—New York, Pennsylvania, New Jersey, and Delaware.

The Delaware is not a spectacular river such as the Columbia system of our northwest, the Fraser of British Columbia or, for that matter, the Mississippi or the Hudson. But the Delaware River system has long been one of the great brown trout, smallmouth bass and walleyed pike resources of our country. And during the early part of the century it was the greatest shad river of them all, when some sixteen million pounds of these silvery fish were harvested each year. Unfortunately, gross pollution in the Philadelphia area all but exterminated this resource and only a skeleton force remains for a possible rebirth.

The gradual meeting of the Delaware with the sea takes place in one of the great estuaries of our Atlantic coast—Delaware Bay. Here is one of the richest shellfish and finfish regions of our nation, and its adjacent salt marshes are both a breeding and wintering grounds of the waterfowl populations of our Atlantic flyway. Here, too, is one of the great natural harbors of our nation, and, like New York Harbor to the north, vessels of the world's commerce come and go around the clock carrying their cargoes of goods and human souls.

So let's take a careful look at this invaluable watershed.

The little hilly and pasture brooklets of the Catskills may flow unnoticed by the average motorist. In fact they may be unknown to most fishermen. But to the countryman and naturalist who fishes for trout and hunts the ruffed grouse, these brooklets have great significance.

These searchers know, for instance, that these tiny streams, which flow through hill and pasture are rich in salamanders, that little known branch of the *Amphibia*. Also, small but brilliantly colored brook trout lurk under the banks, or under the watercress, or under brush or logs in these streams. And these searchers also know that these delicious little fish are timid but can be taken when stealthily approached.

A closer examination of these brooklets will reveal that they run cold—even in the heat of summer—and that their temperatures will seldom exceed 60° F. Such an examination will also reveal that another small fish—the slimy sculpin—is apt to be present. This little-known fish is a gruesome looking creature and a reminder that all life is supposed to have come from the sea. (P.S. It is an excellent bait for brown trout).

As the brooks pick up inflow they become progressively larger and become difficult to cross with a single leap. The water begins to warm slightly and there is a greater variety of aquatic insects under the bottom stones. An occasional small brown trout may be present, together with some small suckers, blacknosed dace and longnosed dace.

The brook has now reached the floor of a small valley or hollow and has become a genuine, small trout stream. Here it may meander a bit through patches of meadow or pasture, alder swamps, old overgrown orchards, and hemlock woods before joining another stream of nearly equal size.

While the brook trout are apt to be larger and the brown trout more numerous in these stretches, the stream is still far too small to attract much attention.

This is unfortunate, because these situations offer a unique and highly rewarding form of contemplative angling. Many country youngsters know about this form of angling and many oldsters—praise God—have neither forgotten nor failed to practice it in later life. Around the "cracker barrel" or in front of a mellow fire it is referred to as "dickie bird fishing", and the art is deserving of detailed description.

The equipment is very simple. Procure a cheap, glass flyrod with plenty of guts and mount any sort of reel at the butt loaded with some nylon line. Attach the end of the line to a foot or two of six or eight pound test monofilament and tie this to a No. 8 or 10, short shanked hook. Then place a split buckshot or small clinch sinker about eight inches above the hook.

Bait is also a simple matter. Dig up some garden hackles (worms) or catch some grasshoppers. (You'd be surprised how many great trout anglers use the latter on the mighty Madison and Snake Rivers of our northwest). But if you become squeamish about this, you can use artificials with success: Get some wet flies in No. 8 or 10 size such as Silver Doctor, Montreal, or Parmachene Belle. Better still, get some McGintys and dip them in a wetting agent. Then rig them as if you were using bait. After all, this is a dunking operation.

Now, having rigged up without landing net or high waders—these are superfluous—put a bottle of insect repellent in your pocket and proceed to the stream sometime in late spring or early summer.

Your approach to the stream must be stealthy: not even a shadow should fall across the water and there must be no thumping from footfalls. Deer paths can often be used to advantage. Follow one of these and crouch low as you view the stream. Peeking carefully through your Polaroid lenses, you note a hole under the bank downstream which is well shadowed by the dense shrubs all around you. Never mind the shrubs, but carefully work the rod tip through a window in them and allow the worm or fly to drift down next to the hole.

Nothing there? Ah! A darting shadow rushes forth from under the bank and grabs the lure. Wait for just a second or so and then hoist mightily; and the chances are that a little stubby brook or brown trout will be wriggling in the shrubbery high above your head. It is your problem how to get it into the creel and proceed to the next hole!

As you work your way downstream you may hear the muffled drumming of a ruffed grouse—or perhaps have one explode from almost beneath your feet. Or you may suddenly realize the silhouette of a deer—skinny and ruddy in its early summer condition—as it watches for your next move.

Above and around you are the songs of birds—the reedy notes of the veery, the staccato chatting of the chipping sparrow, the warbling of a vireo and, perhaps, the pealing tones of the hermit thrush. These are pleasing distractions as you go about your search; and if you are experienced in this business, you will soon have a number of delicious, beautifully colored trout in your creel. To be sure they are small, and to be sure you caught them in a most unorthodox manner. But you had the enjoyable and nourishing experience of

*meeting yourself alone in Nature's kingdom. It can be
an experience that is unforgettable.*

As the stream becomes larger from more inflows,
there are larger and deeper pools and the temperature
rises very gradually. There are more and larger suckers,
and the brown trout all but replaces the brook trout.
Blacknosed dace become more abundant, and small
shiners occasionally flash in the sunlight. Here is temperature at work—temperature and space. For as we
have stated, fishes have particular ranges of temperature preference and tolerance, and space is another factor that is important.

The shallow back-eddies of riffles in streams of this
type are at once important and interesting. For these
are the homes of trout fry—tiny, nervous fish that dart
here and there over the stones and poise with their fins
vibrating. Occasionally, brook, brown, and rainbow
trout fry—which, incidentally, look very much alike—
can be found together in one of these small backwaters.
But brook trout prefer much colder water than browns
or rainbows, and relatively few Catskill streams have
native spawning populations of rainbow trout.

The antics of suckers in the deep, quiet pools are also
interesting. These fish feed upon the organic material—
algae and the tiny animal life it contains—which coat
the stones and bedrock of the stream. And when feeding, the sucker is remindful of a small, animated vacuum
cleaner.

Sometimes the antics of suckers can be downright
heinous. When fly fishing in late summer, for instance,
and when the water is low and gin-clear, the suckers

tend to lurk in the downstream ends of the runs. (The trout, of course, are at the upper ends.) Now, when the run is 50 or 60 feet long, it is necessary to approach the lower end in order to present the dry fly correctly at the upper end where the trout are. And just as you are getting enough line in the air and are about to take that last step or two forward, a batch of big suckers is flushed and proceeds to stampede up to the other end of the run where the trout are. The trout, of course, get the message and they, in turn, panic.

Sometimes we just don't like suckers!

The two great tributaries of the East Branch of the Delaware—the Willowemoc and the Beaverkill—are big trout water. No longer is the backcast a problem, and the rollcast is seldom used. Indeed it is sometimes a problem to wade these streams in order to come within fly casting distance of the target.

These are brown trout streams of the highest quality. The temperatures in summer are in the 70's and high 60's, and the abundance of aquatic insects under the bottom rubble and boulders is something to behold. Wade in anywhere, for instance, and pick up a three-pound stone. The chances are that large mayfly or stone-fly nymphs—perhaps both—will run right up your arm as you examine the underside of the rock. Seldom in eastern North America do you find a stream or river with these conditions. Is it small wonder, then, that these streams, together with the Neversink—another tributary of the Delaware which now does sink—were, before World War II considered by many to be the most priceless brown trout resources of our country?

And what has happened—and what is happening—to this American heritage?

Well, in the first place, Man must have water for his cities, no matter how far he must go for it. So he discovers that the beautiful waters of the Catskills are also beautiful for municipal purposes, and he puts the bulldozers to work and builds huge, beautiful reservoirs. When doing this, Man pays little attention to the homes of fishes. He builds the release works of the reservoir, for instance, in the *hypolimnion* (remember that term?) of the reservoir and fluctuates the releases in a manner that all but ruins the river below for many miles. One day, for example, a small quantity of water is released and warms quickly in the once great river bed. Then, perhaps in a day or two, a large volume of water at 40° F.—far too low for good fishing—pours forth and courses down the stream bed, tearing up the algae that had been growing in the warm water and making a flume out of what was once a great fishery resource. Fortunately, the Beaverkill and the Willowemoc have so far escaped this fate.

Is all this necessary? Definitely not. Man can have his reservoirs without destroying his wildlife legacy—can have his cake and eat it, too—if he is willing to utilize the knowledge he has available and is willing to spend a few more dollars to preserve the American heritage. But let's not get into this very deeply at this time.

Meanwhile, there are more anglers with more automobiles and better highways. Furthermore, many of these anglers now come equipped with spinning gear— a tackle that can make a highly effective angler out of the rankest tyro.

When the East Branch and the West Branch of the Delaware unite at Hancock, N. Y., the river becomes a beautiful, majestic thing which winds its way through the deep, narrow valleys of the Catskills. Here it becomes an excellent smallmouth bass and walleyed pike river: Its bottom is largely rubble and bedrock, and the pools and runs may cover several acres.

It is in this section—hundreds of river miles from the Atlantic Ocean—that one encounters many visitors from the sea. One of them, the sea lamprey—not to be confused with the so-called "landlocked lamprey" of the Great Lakes *—is not a true fish. Rather, it is a large eel-like parasite of marine fishes that ascends rivers to spawn and to die shortly thereafter. But because it somewhat resembles a fish it is best to forget about its absence of jaws and paired fins and just consider it as one.

Anyway, this creature—some of them are three feet long—is very important to Delaware fish and fishermen. Because after the adult lampreys make their trek from the sea, dig out nest depressions in the gravel, spawn and die, the eggs hatch out into things called *larvae*. These larvae—which lack teeth and eyes—dig into underwater mud or sand banks and proceed to grow. And as just about every walleyed pike fisherman on the Delaware knows, these "lamprey eels" are just about tops as bait for walleyes.

It requires about four years for these lamprey larvae to reach a length of about six inches and transform into

---

* Recent evidence suggests that the lake lamprey and the sea lamprey are separate species, and that the latter cannot now permanently "landlock."

the appearance of tiny adults. As soon as they do this, they begin their long journey to the sea, which they apparently complete in a matter of weeks or months. Meanwhile, the careful observer can often spot the presence of lamprey larvae in a sand bank from the habit of these creatures of poking their snouts out above the bottom to feed and remaining in that position for unknown lengths of time.

Another spawning visitor from the sea is the Atlantic shad. This large member of the herring family was long considered to be a commercial net fish only. But in recent years, more and more anglers in other Atlantic coastal rivers have discovered that the shad can be taken on hook and line by casting or trolling and that it is a superb game fish. In fact it is now becoming known as the "poor man's salmon". Each year in the Spring, thousands of anglers journey to the Connecticut River, the Susquehanna, the Potomac and other rivers of our Atlantic coast to fish for shad. Yet here in the Delaware—once the king of them all—only a few adult shad can negotiate the block of pollution down-river, and only a small proportion of the young shad can do likewise as they journey to the sea during late Summer and Autumn.

Still another visitor from the sea is the common eel— abundant to the extent that it is harvested commercially by means of a few specially constructed eel weirs. Of all fishes, the slimy, voracious eel has the most romantic and fantastic life history. Born in the waters of the Atlantic Ocean south of Bermuda, the tiny, glasslike elvers with eyes resembling black dots begin their journey to

Europe or North America. It requires several years to complete the trek, but eventually they reach the mainlands and seek out streams and rivers to ascend.

As they reach the estuaries and tidal portions of the streams, the swarms of elvers become pigmented and begin to resemble miniature, adult eels. And at this point, many—if not most—of the males of the species decide to go no farther. (After all, why push the luck too far?). But most of the females—or so the scientific story goes—are of the adventurous type and proceed to ascend the rivers into fresh water and beyond. In fact they will sometimes proceed for hundreds of miles, follow swamps and trickles, and even go 'cross country a bit on a wet night.

At any rate, these female (?) eels not only conquer the Delaware River, but end up in the most unexpected places—park ponds, farm ponds, and the like. Here, in fresh waters, these eels grow and mature—perhaps in 10 to 15 years—and then attempt to make it back again to the tropical waters of the Atlantic Ocean. The males, of course, which have been supposedly spending their time in the brackish water, have it much easier. Oh, well. . . .

While the visitors from the sea may be the most romantic of the Delaware River fishes, the smallmouth bass and the walleyed pike are the bread-and-butter items for the angler. And as the Delaware becomes larger and slower it forms an increasingly favorable home for these and other warmwater species—more than 75 in all. Even the lowly carp breaches the surface of the huge, deep pools and runs, and the outboard motor soon replaces waders as a means to the end.

Below Port Jervis, where three states—New York, Pennsylvania, and New Jersey meet—powered craft are a common sight.

Bass fishing in this region of the Delaware can become a rather specialized affair. One of the special baits, for instance, is the little stonecat—a member of the catfish family that lives under flat pieces of rubble and boulder. We shall never forget our first exposure to the preferred method of procuring this bait: We saw a man wading along the shore and pounding stones with a big sledge hammer. The purpose, it seems, was to stun the stonecat by concussion and then pick up the fish as it drifted downstream. Oh, yes . . . The method was very effective.

Nor shall we ever forget the interview we had many years ago with a native who spent many hours in his anchored rowboat and who caught many big smallmouths. He, too, had a system. "The whole secret, Son," he said, "is to wait long enough when they grab the minnow. Now some people may argue this, but I wait three minutes. I put my watch down on the seat in front of me and I time it. Yessir, it takes three whole minutes for that bass to get the minnow down into him!"

The section of the river between Port Jervis and the famous Delaware Water Gap represents one of the most unusual paradoxes of our nation and times: Here, within two or three hours' driving time from New York City, Philadelphia, and the sprawling megalopolis of this region of our country, is one of the finest and most underutilized smallmouth bass and walleyed pike resources of eastern North America. While hordes of anglers fish almost elbow to elbow for recently stocked trout in tributary streams, the Delaware flows deep and wild through the wooded hills of northern Pennsylvania and New Jersey. Fishermen are few and far between.

Perhaps it is the very bigness and wildness of this portion of the Delaware that accounts for the paradox. After all, the city angler who fishes for "put and take" trout next to a highway may find the spectacle of the Delaware far too challenging for his time, knowledge and desires. It could be so.

The eastern chain pickerel becomes more abundant in these slower regions of the Delaware, although it seldom compares in size with the pickerel of nearby lakes. A 20-inch fish is a prize in the Delaware, while 28-inch pickerel, weighing six pounds or more, are not uncommon in nearby lakes.

The stretch of the river between Delaware Water Gap and Trenton, N. J., although quite picturesque, is not something to raise the blood pressure of the "old pro" angler: The river becomes almost clumsy in its flow, there is much mud bottom, and the evidences of flooding in the broad agricultural plains is apparent. To be sure, there are big walleyes and smallmouths and pickerel here, and there are many bullheads and even channel catfish; but there is no extravaganza such as exists upstream.

Yet this stretch of the Delaware is very important to the angler and the conservationist. Because, before the cancer of pollution was allowed to strike the tidal portions of the Delaware, these waters were part of the spawning grounds of the striped bass—that highly prized gamefish of the Atlantic and Pacific coasts. It is unfortunate that food and game fishes such as the shad and the striper are unable to take it (pollution) in the manner of the parasitic lamprey.

At Trenton, the Delaware River descends to tidal water in boiling rapids. Some anglers and conservationists who like to see symbols in such things, claim that the river is simply recapitulating its youth before contributing its body in the form of nutrients to a great marine estuary below.

Be this as it may. The fact remains that the Delaware —as all other rivers—will be constantly reborn and replenished through the hydrologic cycle. It will continue to be a haunt of fish and fishermen so long as man shall use it wisely.

5   The Fish at Home
In Oceans, Bays, and Estuaries

The whole world is just an ocean—barring, of course, some "islands" that protrude from the surface.

—An oceanographer

Almost all maps of continents and islands portray the boundaries of these natural phenomena as ending at the water's edge. Political speeches have referred to the "rock bound coasts of Maine" and the "sunny shores of California". Even the territorial waters' limit of three nautical miles is based upon the effective firing range of a cannon some centuries ago. We are a land-minded nation.

Fortunately for both fishes and people, land masses do not end at the water's edge but extend as submerged land for varying distances. Sometimes the distance is small—less than a mile—while in other instances the submerged land extends for more than 200 miles before dropping steeply into the deep abysses of the sea. These extensive areas are called "continental shelves", and our own continent is blessed with both an Atlantic shelf and a Pacific shelf in its more northern latitudes, and a third, of lesser size, in the Gulf of Mexico.

These shallow areas of the sea are the homes of most of our marine food and game fishes. To be sure, many of the big-game fishes—the broadbill swordfish, the tunas and the marlins—are cosmopolitan and roam the high seas. But name the "bread-and-butter" species that are important to most saltwater anglers and commercial fishermen, and almost all will be found to be inhabitants of the shore regions or the continental shelves.

There are definite reasons for this. In the first place, these waters receive quantities of nutrients—particularly nitrates and phosphates—from the land, which are transported to the ocean by rivers. And these nutrients, as we have seen, are vital to the production of plant plankton—the tiny microscopic plant life in the water and upon which all other aquatic life depends, including animal plankton.

In the second place, light, which is essential for the production of this microscopic plant life in the water, can penetrate these depths.

And finally, the bottom—and most particularly rough bottom—is the home of many marine animals upon which fishes feed. The result? A highly productive situation for fish life.

Both the Atlantic and Pacific continental shelves of North America begin to assume major proportions in the mid-latitudes of United States—the former to a much greater degree than the latter—and become more and more extensive toward the northeast and northwest. In fact, both of these shelves are so broad in their northern regions that they have become a subject of international discussions. After all, who owns what? Who should have priority, etc.?

The important food and game fishes that occur in these vast marine areas have been grouped into three convenient categories: (1) groundfishes—those that live on or very near the bottom; (2) shorefishes—those that live in the bays, estuaries or not far from shore; and (3) pelagic fishes—those that roam the sea without dependency upon bottom dwelling organisms.

Now, before we consider these types of fishes and the particular homes and habits of many species of each type, we should perhaps relax a bit and try to prepare ourselves for the immensity of our subject. For we are no longer considering the trout that's here and there in the running stream, the big muskie in the cove, or even schools of walleyes, yellow perch or ciscos in the Great Lakes. On the contrary, we are now considering vast, productive areas of moving salt water where moving fish populations are measured in the millions and billions of individuals or pounds. If, therefore, we were formerly thinking in terms of a six-inch ruler, let us now be prepared to think in terms of the surveyor's tape.

> *The sky o'erarches here, we feel the undulating deck beneath our feet,*
> *We feel the long pulsation, ebb and flow of endless motion.*
> *The tones of unseen mystery, the vague and vast suggestions of the briny world. . . .*
>
> Walt Whitman

The important groundfishes of the Pacific continental

shelf include halibut—that delicious monster flatfish that seems to be on the menu of most American restaurants and diners—flounders, cod, lingcod, sablefish, and more than three dozen species of rockfishes.

The chief groundfishes of the Atlantic shelf are cod, haddock, flounders—including blackback or winter flounder, fluke or summer flounder—whiting, ling or red or squirrel hake, pollack or Boston bluefish, and rosefish or ocean "perch" or red "perch".

Perhaps the best way to describe the homes of these various species of groundfishes is to portray a section of the continental shelf of our north Atlantic coast and to indicate how depth and the type of bottom are important factors in determining where these homes are. In fact, in order to do this, we are using an illustration that has been copied from one of the most informative and valuable documents on fishery resources that we've seen.*

Now, after having examined this illustration very carefully, let's study the middle Atlantic section of our coast so that we can examine matters more closely and orient them to why fish bite and why they don't.

This map shows one of the busiest commercial fishing areas—and certainly the busiest marine angling region of its size—in the world. In fact, saltwater angling has become big business in this area, where thousands of fishing craft carry more than a million anglers each year for the purpose of catching fish that bite. In addition there are the many thousands of privately owned craft

---

* Fishery Resources of the United States. Senate Document No. 51, 79th Congress, 1st Session. (For sale by the Superintendent of Documents, U. S. Government Printing Office, Washington, D.C.).

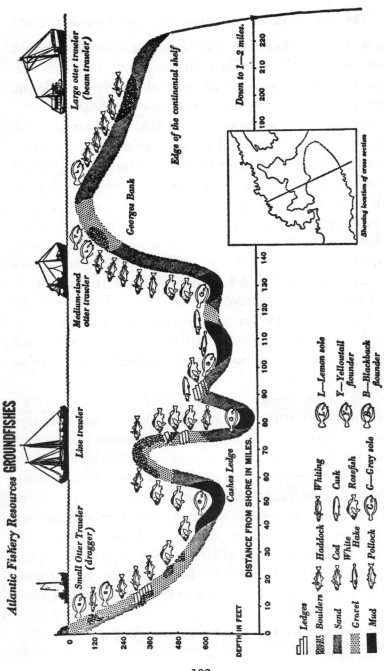

Atlantic Fishery Resources GROUNDFISHES

CROSS SECTION OF THE GULF OF MAINE, SHOWING DISTRIBUTION OF GROUNDFISH BY DEPTH AND TYPE OF BOTTOM.

Small Otter Trawler (dragger)

Line trawler

Medium-sized otter trawler

Large otter trawler (beam trawler)

Cashes Ledge

Georges Bank

Edge of the continental shelf

Down to 1—2 miles.

DEPTH IN FEET

DISTANCE FROM SHORE IN MILES.

Ledges
Boulders
Sand
Gravel
Mud

L—Lemon sole
Y—Yellowtail flounder
B—Blackback flounder
G—Grey sole

Haddock
Cod
White Hake
Pollock

Whiting
Cusk
Rosefish

Showing location of cross section

102

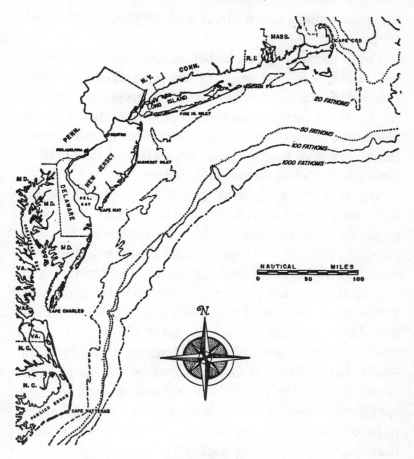

and the other thousands of surf anglers—that special, frustrated breed of angler who carries eternal hope in his breast.

The waters of our middle Atlantic coast are considerably warmer than those of our north Atlantic above Cape Cod—as bathers will quickly testify. And the former has an abundance of all three groups of fishes: the groundfishes, shorefishes and the pelagic group. So let's consider the important species of each category and observe how these move about and go through their life cycles.

The important groundfishes, insofar as the angler is concerned, are the fluke or summer flounder, *Paralichthys dentatus*, the sea bass, *Centropristes striatus*, the northern porgy, *Stenotomus chrysops*, the winter or blackback flounder, *Pseudopleuronectes americanus*, the blackfish or tautog, *Tautoga onitis*, and the northern blowfish or puffer, *Sphaeroides maculatus*.

The first three of these groundfishes—the fluke, sea bass and porgy—have somewhat similar migratory movements in the middle Atlantic region of the continental shelf: all three move close to shore and into the bays and estuaries during spring, remain for the summer, and then slowly migrate eastward and southward to the outer regions of the shelf. There is some indication, however—and this is one of the things that makes marine fisheries research so challenging and interesting—that there may be at least a more northern and a more southern group or population segment of each of these species, and that these population segments may be partially or wholly independent of each other. (We warned that this subject is complicated!)

There are other complexities. Tagging experiments, for instance, have indicated that fluke, having once migrated with the seasons, tend to follow precisely the same itinerary the following year—even to the extent of returning to the same bars. And there is evidence that some sea bass change their sex as they become older. But again . . . shall we quit while we're ahead?

During summer, many fluke have a tendency to lurk on sand bars in inlets, and in the channels of bays and estuaries. Most, however, tend to remain at sea but within a few miles of shore.

Porgies and sea bass have a great affinity for rocky bottoms and old, sunken wrecks at depths of 30 to 80 feet during summer. The porgy has a tendency to lurk a foot or more above the bottom, while the sea bass prefers to be closer to his work.

The winter or blackback flounder has a large number of populations or population segments. In fact each bay or estuary is apt to have its own. These fish enter these inshore regions during autumn, remain more or less dormant during the coldest part of winter, and then start feeding voraciously as the sunlight becomes brighter and the water temperatures rise a few degrees. Spawning also takes place at this time and the flounders usually conduct this operation on the bars or flats.

As the days become longer and the waters continue gradually to warm, the flounders begin to move along the channels towards the sea. It is at this time—usually during April and May—that they can be taken in very large numbers, and few—if any fishes—surpass the winter flounder in flavor. In fact, the flatfishes—flounders, halibuts and soles—are among the tastiest of fishes, and perhaps something should be mentioned about their strange "deformity", which takes place early in life.

When first hatched from the egg, the flatfishes greatly resemble other fishes: There is an eye on each side of the head and they swim in the conventional, upright manner. But within a matter of days or weeks, a change occurs that destines the flatfish to swim on its side for the remainder of its life: one of the eyes begins to migrate over the top of the creature's head to a position along-side the other eye. When this takes place, the eyed side becomes darkly pigmented while the other remains white. Seems a bit awkward, doesn't it? Yet far from being a disadvantage, the flatfish is then the better to ambush and stalk its prey! In some species the left eye migrates over to the right side and the species is known as a "right eyed" one. In others it is vice versa.

The tautog or blackfish is one of the most paradoxical of our marine fishes. In New England, where the former name prevails, it is considered an excellent food and game fish; southward it is usually not considered to be much of either. To illustrate the paradox still further, the species is far more common along the rocky New England coast than farther to the south, and such abundance usually makes the heart less fond.

But there are very significant reasons for this state of affairs—reasons that the freshwater angler who has never seen the sea may well appreciate. They have to do with clear blue running water and rocks and ledges; with islands and expanses of water shining in the sunlight; and with big strong fish lurking here and there, which are difficult to hook when they bite. They may be in ten feet of water or in 30.

Contrast this with an open expanse of ocean where the species may be 100 feet down and when it may require eight ounces of lead to hold the bottom. (Shades of lake trout and landlocked salmon during mid-summer!). Yet this is the contrast between catching tautog in New England, and blackfish—the same species—in the open ocean to the west and south.

And the flavor? Well, there's more to this than meets

the taste buds of the tongue; and that which is originally appreciated may receive greater attention in further use.

The northern blowfish or puffer is the clown fish of the region. This is due to its ability to swell many times its size with air or water. When fully distended, it presents such a whimsical spectacle that one wonders about the cause of it all. Actually, this is a defense mechanism, rather than any sort of jet pump for digging mollusks and other food out of the bottom as might be surmised.

Blowfish are excellent table fare, despite the fact that many anglers who do not know the eight-second method of cleaning them consider the species a nuisance. At the market place they are known as sea chicken or sea squab, and commercial fishermen appreciate their value. In fact, it was while on a commercial bay boat that we first learned how blowfish spawn, and we'd like to report it here for the first time:

It was about five o'clock on a June morning out near the center of Great South Bay, Long Island. The surface of the water was a glassy sheen, and the fishing boat chugged along slowly as it made its way toward Fire Island Inlet, leaving a very long wake on the still waters. Every once in awhile, one could see something rippling the surface and moving along slowly.

Finally, we caught sight of a group of blowfish cruising at the top in an echelon formation. In the lead was a large blowfish—obviously a female—followed by a half dozen smaller fish which were apparently males. Nothing happened while we were able to watch this group, nor as we watched several other echelons.

Then, as we observed still another group, the fish went into a flurry of activity. We could only conclude that they were spawning, with all the males trying to get into the act. Perhaps more than one male did, and, by providing more sperm in the water, assured a more fertile spawning.

Blowfish move into and out of bays and estuaries with the seasons much in the manner of winter flounders: *in* during autumn and *out* during late spring and early summer.

Among the many shorefishes of the middle Atlantic coast are a number of game species. These include the weakfish or sea trout or gray trout or squeteague, the croaker, the striped bass or rock, and the bluefish. All of these species go through periods of abundance and scarcity over the years. Sometimes these fluctuations are far apart—a decade or more—and sometimes they take place from one year to the next. The latter instance usually occurs when the species suddenly becomes abundant from a highly successful spawning, while the former is usually the result of a gradual reduction from natural and fishing mortality.

It seems questionable, however, whether the weakfish will ever reach its former average size while under the present conditions of fishing pressure. This species spawns in the bays and estuaries of the middle Atlantic coast. The young that are spawned in the northern section migrate to the southern section—particularly to the region of Chesapeake Bay—at the end of their first summer when they are only a few inches long. The young that are spawned in the southern region, on the other hand, simply remain there for their first winter.

Now, if the northern spawned youngsters had any sense of Yankee loyalty they would certainly all return north after spending their first winter in more southern climes. But no! They usually choose to remain for just one more year. Perhaps the Yankee weakfish are merely trying to persuade their Dixie brethren to journey north with them, because this is just what a large proportion of the southern "weaks" do when two years old.

Anyway, it's all too late, because during their second summer of life, the weakfish reach "eating size" and are harvested in tremendous numbers. After all, this is truly a case of the "bird in hand being worth two in the bush". And the result? While there is plenty of weakfish, there is not much opportunity for the species to reach the "tiderunner" or "yellowfin" size of several pounds, which it used to do so abundantly in the past.

The croaker, a member of the same family as the weakfish, is a Dixiecrat to begin with and there is no justifiable reason for us Yankees to get excited over its scarcity north of Maryland. Indeed it is only in years of superabundance that the species "spills over" into New Jersey; and even during such times it is seldom abundant as far north as Long Island.

As for the striped bass or striper or rock, well now, here we have a really difficult one. In the first place, it has become the symbol—emotional and otherwise—of the growing marine angling interests on the Atlantic coast and, particularly, the middle Atlantic coast. In the second place, it is an anadromous fish—one that ascends rivers to spawn—with a life history and population phenomena so complex that some 25 years of research by many persons and conservation agencies has yielded findings that only marine fishery scientists and a minority of anglers seem able to comprehend, believe and appreciate. Anyway, here is the story.

The striped bass is born (hatched from an egg) in the fresh waters of certain rivers. At one time, it would appear, nearly all the rivers of our Atlantic coast contained striped bass, just as many of our more northern rivers contained salmon. But as in the case of the Atlantic salmon, most—in fact, nearly all—of these rivers were polluted, dammed, dredged or bulkheaded to such an extent that the areas necessary for successful spawning were either seriously damaged or totally destroyed. Fortunately, most of the major spawning rivers of the striped bass, while damaged, remained in a condition that was adequate for the survival and abundant supply of the species. These include certain rivers of Chesapeake Bay, and the Hudson River. Practically gone, however, are the spawning grounds of the mighty Delaware.

The result of all this is that probably more than 80

per cent of the striped bass of our middle Atlantic coast come from the Chesapeake. The Hudson River, to be sure, contributes locally, but its over-all contribution is negligible.

We now come to the second set of remarkable facts about the striper. Researches have revealed, for instance, that most stripers never migrate from the rivers of their birth or the adjacent bays and that of those that do, the female is more venturesome than the male, and travels much farther. The researches also reveal that up-river bass which, apparently seldom if ever see the sea, can be landlocked successfully.

Finally, there is the third set of facts. When stripers migrate along our coast—northward in spring and southward in autumn—they do so rather steadily and rapidly. In other words, the seasonal abundance along most shorelines is very short-lived. When stripers "settle" for the summer, they prefer sheltered areas and special situations—rocky bottom, pilings, jetties, sounds and islands. And when they are ensconced in such situations, the average surf angler is just about wasting his time. For when sojourning in such summer homes, the striper is difficult to locate and to entice. As one dedicated striper fishing friend once put it:

"You have to discover dynamic situations, which develop within a radius of ten feet or less under certain conditions of time and tide—usually at night. Then you must present the correct lure or bait in just the right manner—sometimes again and again. But if you are able to do all this, you can catch them again and again!"

We should perhaps mention here that while the striper is one of the greatest of our challenge fishes, its fighting qualities leave something to be desired. In fact, one of our fishing colleagues once admitted that the greatest fight he ever encountered while surf fishing was from a four foot plank that he hooked while casting at Montauk Point, Long Island. (P.S. He still fishes for stripers there).

Of all the middle Atlantic fishes—or for that matter of all fishes—the bluefish is perhaps the greatest. Very little is known about this species, but researches to date indicate that it is a warmwater species with a rapid growth rate. Where bluefish come from or where they go, on our Atlantic coast, is still a mystery.

Bluefish usually invade the waters of the middle Atlantic during May, and there appear to be two or three —perhaps more—waves of invasion. And by the end of summer, they have left an appealing calling card in the form of swarms of young bluefish in our bays and estuaries. These young bluefish, called snappers or snapper blues, grow to a length of ten inches or so before leaving around the autumnal Equinox, and they can provide some excellent flyrod fishing, and eating.

The prowling, savage adults also invade the bays and estuaries on occasion, and provide the rowboat anglers with some superb fishing.

As for ocean angling, this species is without parallel: it strikes savagely with its razor sharp teeth, fights ferociously with great strength and unpredictable versatility, and never gives up until death has invaded its body. And it occasionally reaches a weight of 20 pounds! We have sometimes wondered how the great hordes of bluefish that frequently haunt our Atlantic coast can possibly survive without depleting all other smaller species. But they fail to do this, such is the immense productivity of the sea.

It was during the month of June that an executive of the Great Beach park called on the phone to complain about the dead fish. "Doctor," he said, "the entire Beach is strewn with cut fish. Putting pieces of the fish together, it seems that these are menhaden [one of the most prolific members of the herring family] and that the commercial fishermen who caught them cut their livers out and threw them overboard. They have now drifted up onto the Beach and it's a terrible mess!"

"This is impossible," we replied. "Commercial fishermen who purse seine for menhaden never cut them. They sell them whole to a reduction plant which renders them into oil and fishmeal. Sounds to me like the work of bluefish. There are schools of them along the Beach, you know."

"Impossible, Doctor, the bluefish along the Beach are only about 12 inches long and most of these menhaden must be at least 10 inches. They are cut right in two."

"But have you ever seen the work of bluefish? Sometimes they'll chase a school of fish right up onto the beach—killing, chopping and slashing. The size difference you mention doesn't bar this possibility."

"You don't say, Doctor. But would you come out and see this situation for yourself?"

(P.S. We did and that's just what it was.)

The importance of the bays and estuaries of the middle Atlantic coast should not be underestimated; for most of the economically important fishes of this area

of the continental shelf are dependent upon these inshore waters during some stage of their life cycles.
Sometimes it is for spawning; sometimes as a nursery
area for young; sometimes for both. The waters of these
inshore resources are brackish to varying degrees, and
are rich in nutrients from land run-off. This, together
with physical shelter, provides an abundance of food
and protection for these young fishes.

The pelagic gamefishes of the middle Atlantic area
include the Atlantic or "Boston" mackerel, the chub or
thimble-eye mackerel, bonito, the bluefin tuna, the false
or autumn albacore, the white marlin and the broadbill
swordfish. Occasionally a blue marlin is seen or cap-
tured.

Atlantic mackerel and chub mackerel prefer to remain in the waters of the continental shelf, although
both species regularly roam into the waters of the north
Atlantic. The tuna, marlin and broadbill, however, reside for the most part outside shelf waters—either in the
Gulf Stream or marginal waters—and move in only during summer. In fact it would seem that only relatively
small numbers of some of these species do this, and on
a most unpredictable basis.

Of these several game fishes, only the Atlantic mackerel has a life history that is known and it is a very interesting one. The Atlantic mackerel, it would appear,
spends the winter out near the edge of the southern portion of the middle Atlantic, continental shelf—probably
in a semi-dormant condition some distance from the
bottom.

During April the species begins to shake its winter
lethargy and swims toward shore and then northeast-

ward. By the middle or end of May it is ready to spawn in the waters of the middle Atlantic coast and then move on into the north Atlantic. Countless trillions of buoyant eggs are broadcast into the sea at this time, and a difference as little as *two ten-thousandths of one per cent* in the survival of these eggs into mackerel can account for a bumper crop or a poor one! In other words, the mortality of the eggs may vary between 99.9996% and 99.9998% (or less) and this variation, it would appear, is due primarily to physical, chemical and biological conditions of the water at the time of spawning and shortly thereafter. Conditions can be even worse, when only four newly spawned mackerel out of one million survive for as little as three months! Is it small wonder, then, that the mackerel, like many other marine fishes, varies greatly in abundance over the years?

Mackerel are plankton feeders and have special devices on the insides of their gill arches for straining animal plankton from the sea. This is why they are found in mid-water or at the surface during the warmer seasons. The fact that mackerel will strike and devour much larger organisms has nothing to do with this special apparatus. They also have large mouths with small teeth.

And at approximately what depth do Atlantic mackerel usually lurk at this time? Well, why not try approximately 30 feet?

The big-game fishes of the middle Atlantic coast—the tuna, false albacore, white marlin and occasional blue marlin—are not natives of the continental shelf. Little is known about the life histories of these fishes,

but apparently they reside, for the most part, in the Gulf Stream east and south of the shelf or in closely adjacent waters. During summer, unknown proportions invade the shelf waters and come fairly close to shore for reasons equally unknown.

This brings us to other homes of marine fishes, such as major ocean currents and "upwellings". The famous Gulf Stream, for instance, is one example of a major current, and the cold but equally famous Humboldt Current off South America is another. "Upwellings" are vertical currents that bring waters rich in chemical nutrients from the depths up into surface waters. They may occur both within ocean currents and in certain other areas of the sea.

Contrary to popular belief, it is the cold ocean currents, upwellings, and adjacent waters that are the most productive of fish poundage. In fact, the cold Humboldt Current, which flows northward along the coasts of Chile and Peru, is probably the richest ocean current in the world. It is aquamarine in "color" and slightly turbid from plankton, in contrast to the clear blue of the Gulf Stream of the Atlantic. The reason again is the quantity of dissolved plant nutrients—especially phosphorus—in the water, and this is why the great fish producing areas of the world usually happen to be the cooler regions of the sea and where these meet warmer waters. The Humboldt Current, incidentally, which is sometimes more than four miles deep, flows close to shore far up into the tropics and doesn't begin to flow westward until it has reached a latitude of about 8° South.

Just as the south Pacific has its Humboldt or "Peruvian" Current, so does the north Pacific have its cold Oyashio and California Currents, the north Atlantic its Labrador, the south Atlantic its Benguela, etc. And when these cold currents meet with warm currents or other warmer waters, upwellings from the rich depths occur with the consequent "fertilization" of the surface waters.

Warm ocean currents may also carry an abundance of dissolved nutrients in their depths—sometimes more so than cold currents—and this may raise the question of which comes first "the chicken or the egg?" The Gulf Stream, for example is rich in nutrients down deep; but the Gulf Stream has to travel a long way before it encounters enough cold water to cause major upwellings. These occur, however, when this warm current collides with the Labrador Current of the north Atlantic.

Upwellings can also occur from wind action, when deep water rises to replace surface water that has been blown away by winds. This is continually occurring—from minor to major extents—in the sea, and one can often witness one example of it on a bathing beach during offshore winds: the warm surface water is blown seaward and is replaced by colder water.

It might be asked at this point why the depths of the sea are so rich in chemical nutrients and how they got there in the first place? The answer is rather simple: when plant and animal plankton complete their short life cycles and die, their remains shower downward and decompose from bacterial action. This produces "fertilizer" just as other organic material does when it "rots" or decomposes. In fact the tiny "shells" of certain animal plankton are deposited to unknown thicknesses at the bottom in the depths of the sea and are called "oozes". Now these "oozes" . . . but here we go again!

Returning to the Humboldt Current and adjacent waters, this is one of the most underutilized ocean fishery resources of the world. Here one can see square miles of yellowfin tuna; square miles of anchovies feeding upon "surface drift"; bonito in untold numbers; world record broadbill swordfish, black and striped marlin, which feed upon the abundant giant squid or "jibia". And as if this were not enough, the guano birds and gannets feed from above while the Humboldt penguins feed from below. Here, surely, is a fisherman's paradise . . .

The little trawler with the short bow pulpit was on an observation trip. No one aboard had any big-game angling equipment and the iron (harpoon) that was available left much to be desired. The "dirty" water of the Humboldt was several miles astern and we were in the calm blue waters of the Pacific west of Antofagasta, Chile. The boat smelled like all small "draggers" any-where—a mixture of Diesel oil and stale fish. It can be a pleasant smell to those who know it.

"Cookie"—a short man of light stature—was busily engaged in peeling onions that he pulled, one by one, from a long string of them hanging from the outside of the deckhouse. We were busy watching "Cookie" at his work and wondering what sort of concoction he was preparing.

Suddenly, "Cookie" looked up and his eyes became transfixed by something out on the ocean. "Albacora"! he screamed, as he leaped from the box he had been sitting on, "Albacora"! He started to run towards the bow, but his bare feet went out from under him on the slippery deck and he took a real spill. Undaunted, "Cookie" scrambled up quickly, pointed, and yelled again at the top of his voice. "Albacora"!

Sure enough, we sighted the stiff, arched fins of a broadbill about 200 yards away. This was no 200 pounder lolling half asleep at the surface off Block Island in the Atlantic. This brute was at least 500 and was cruising about slowly.

Approaches were in vain. We put him down as we did several others. All told, we sighted 18 broadbill swordfish within an hour and a half, and one of these great fish with the saucer eyes must have weighed close to a thousand pounds. When he sounded, the wake was awesome to behold.

Perhaps it made no difference whether or not we had "stuck" one on this expedition. With the type of keg and line we had aboard, the broadbill might well have sounded to great depths and have smashed the keg with water pressure.

Broadbill strike a bait very readily in these waters, and the reason is their habit of feeding upon the abundant, giant squid or "jibia". These squid are several feet long and seem to lurk near the thermocline (remember that term?) of the sea, but they will often readily come to the surface. If a hook is baited with the head and tentacles of one of these gruesome creatures and is correctly presented, there's a good chance of the swordfish striking it. Indeed, the late W. E. S. Tuker of Tocopilla, Chile, once holder of the world's record for broadbill, told us that about one out of every two would strike this bait. "In fact", he said, "it was so easy that I began to use a rigged bonito in order to make it more challenging." (P.S. Are you listening out there at Montauk?)

Needless to say, we have long regretted the nearly 5,000 miles that separate us from the Humboldt Current and the land of violent earthquakes, wonderful people and fine music. But even as the far-off places may have a special appeal, so too, do certain places close to home. One of these, for instance, is a home for marine fishes the like of which we have never seen anywhere, including the Humboldt Current.

This is the area between Montauk Point, Long Island, and Cape Cod, Massachusetts. Here we have just about everything that the saltwater angler can dream about—broadbill swordfish, white marlin, tuna, bonito, mackerel, striped bass, flounder, fluke, bluefish, tautog, porgies (scup), weakfish (squeteague), cod, tomcod, hake, pollack, sea bass, and blowfish. There are bays, estuaries, rocks, islands, sounds, and the open sea. And there are lobsters, blue crabs, clams (quahogs) and oysters.

They are all there, untarnished and practically untouched. And there is the "long pulsation, ebb and flow of endless motion. The tones of unseen mystery, the vague and vast suggestions of the briny world . . .".

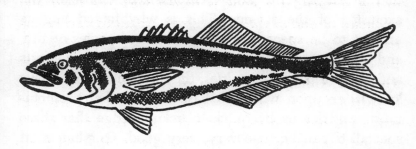

6   The Art and the Science
Of Fishing

Nature, to be commanded,
must be obeyed.
— Francis Bacon

The practice of medicine—whether veterinary or human—is often described as an art based upon a science. The same definition applies to angling, except that in angling the art is emphasized almost to the exclusion of the science. This is why famed anglers are apt to be specialists for one or two species of fish, and often in limited situations. By devoting their efforts and study to such specialties, they obtain the necessary knowledge upon which to base their skilled presentations. And let us be quick to acknowledge that these specialists can become very, very good. Our hat is off to them.

But transport these anglers to a variety of situations—lakes, ponds, rivers, streams, oceans, bays and estuaries —and the chances are that the proficiency will be absent due to lack of knowledge. In fact these anglers, being dedicated to a specialty, might find the entire proceedings quite boring.

The same holds true for so-called "native guides". By spending many years on a particular lake or group of lakes, they gain sufficient knowledge to work out some fairly consistent procedures and methods for catching fish. Yet few have an accurate knowledge of the depth contours and types of bottom of these lakes, nor the characteristics of their thermal stratifications. And they may be entirely unaware of highly effective angling techniques that are being used in other lakes as little as fifty or a hundred miles away.

Here again we have no desire to discredit. Many of these guides are keen, professional students of the game, and it can be a joy to talk shop with them and compare notes to mutual benefit. Furthermore, these craftsmen of the outdoors are indispensable to those many anglers who would be at a loss—and perhaps a dangerous one—without the knowledge and skill of these professional guides.

The point that we are attempting to make here is that there exists a great body of knowledge—a science—

upon which the art of angling can be based, and that this science is not limited to particular situations. It can be used in entirely new ones—even in strange countries—and it can bring to the angler moments of truth that are especially rewarding.

The trim, hydrographic yacht Vidal Gormaz, *of the Chilean Navy had anchored in the Bay of Mas a Tierra —the so-called "Robinson Crusoe" island of the Juan Fernández pair—some 300 miles off the coast of Chile. (Mas a Tierra is called Robinson Crusoe's island, because it was here that Alexander Selkirk, the prototype hero of Daniel Defoe's immortal story, lived in solitude for more than four years).*

Night had fallen and the special lights over the side of the ship illuminated the rippling blue water below. One could see a school of fish swimming lazily at the surface and gulping, from time to time, in the manner of goldfish. But these were obviously members of the jack family (Carangidae) and would run about two or three pounds.

No casting rod was available, but we had a fresh-water baitcasting reel in our tackle box loaded with black nylon line. Attaching a leader to the line, and a small clamp sinker, we tied on a yellow and red buck-tail—the forerunner of the Micky Finn—paid out some line and, swinging the sinker in circles, threw the buck-tail out about 50 feet and began to bring it in hand over hand. A jack seized it almost immediately and we added one more species to the list of 30 fishes that this lure had taken in fresh and salt waters—a lure that had

*been originally designed for smallmouth bass in Ontario
and upper New York State!*

While this account may come as no surprise to many
anglers, it should be revealed that the particular event
took place some 16 years ago, or long before the broad
effectiveness of spinning gear and lures had given rise
to a somewhat more general approach to various game
fishes. It might also be mentioned, in passing, that the
chief factors responsible for the effectiveness of spin
fishing—less visibility of line and long retrieve of light
lures—were well known by a few anglers many years
before the widespread adoption of spinning gear. These
anglers fashioned their own, five or six-foot bait-casting
tips and learned to cast as little as one-eighth ounce.
Some of them even learned the importance of precision
action in a spinner and would comb the tackle shops
in search of such a one. In those days, of course, it was
considered unsportsmanlike to use this type of gear in
trout streams.

Before considering some fundamental principles that
can be used in getting fish to bite, a few words should
be said about technical skill. Let's be honest about
this. The technical command of an instrument can be
as important to the angler as it is to the musician, the
surgeon, or the baseball player. To be sure, such
methods as spinning, trolling and bait fishing require
far less manual technique than fly casting or bait casting—and are far less rewarding—but technique is still
a very important matter. Yet technique would be sterile
without the necessary knowledge to guide it, and this
is why we emphasize the mental aspects of the art and

the science. As the noted angler and outdoor writer, Jason Lucas, once pointed out to an inquiring reader, the most valuable piece of equipment an angler has is "his head".

In our chapter on the fish in person, certain factors other than hunger were described as having a great deal to do with why fish bite. These included competition (including the bullying urge), conditioning or preconditioning, water agitation, etc. In other words, there are factors other than hunger that can stimulate or "trigger" a fish to strike a bait or lure, and these account for the two general approaches—or philosophies—in angling. One of these is *imitation* of natural food, or the use of it; the other is based upon *exaggeration*. Sometimes both are combined—often unwittingly. So let's examine each of these approaches and their combinations.

The best example of the *imitation* approach is the "match the hatch" method of the dryfly trout fisherman. He studies the aquatic insects that are "hatching" at the time and imitates them from a large inventory of exquisitely tied artificials that he usually carries on his person.

The *exaggeration* approach, on the other hand, is probably best exemplified by the myriad of "gollywoggle" and other brightly colored lures that one sees displayed in most tackle stores. Has a fish ever seen anything like them? We doubt it. Yet some of them are highly effective and there is a reason. Fish, for example, have been shown to respond to gross exaggerations of certain phenomena much more quickly and intensely than to normal manifestations of these phenomena The sexual behavior of a male fish, for example, may be greatly stimulated by gross exaggerations of certain sexual characteristics, or behavior, of the female. Grotesque distensions of the belly of a model, exaggerations of color, or posed position—all these have been found to be particularly effective.

Is it small wonder, then, that some of the most outlandish contraptions are very effective in getting fish to bite? Or that what may be highly effective in one situation may be equally so in a number of others?

Now, before we may pooh-pooh all this or begin to laugh at the fish, let's consider *Homo sapiens* for a moment. For instance, let's examine the mannequins in the windows of our dress shops—artificial models that display dresses designed to get the female of the species to bite. Measure the hips and other features of these mannequins. Do the measurements come out anything like 36-24-36? Heavens, no! In fact, if you took the hip measurements to an obstetrician he, or she, would probably either stare at them in disbelief or prepare for a Caesarian.

This, of course, is a case of negative exaggeration. But let us absorb our lesson in humility and get back to the fish.

The chief difficulty in the exaggeration approach is the lack of scientific determinations of what features should be exaggerated and the degree of the exaggeration. This is unfortunate, because it remains a fertile field for research which could bring much edification and enjoyment to mankind. (And what other justification is there for scientific research?)

Despite this lack, however, some rhyme and reason

have emerged from the free-for-all of lure manufacture. A combination of red and yellow or red and white, for instance, is highly attractive to most, if not all, gamefishes; the actions of bucktail hair, hackle feathers, and "Marabou" feathers (usually from a white turkey) are also effective across the board; and highly polished surfaces of metallic lures are apparently less effective than ."scale" or dull finishes. Black or other darkly colored lures, including red—which appears dark in the absence of much light—are highly effective at night when passing over the fish; and precision action in spinners is also highly important, particularly to freshwater game fishes.

Here we have an interesting mystery. If, as it would appear, spinners are more attractive to freshwater gamefishes than to saltwater forms, why is this so? What feature peculiar to freshwater life is the spinner representing and exaggerating? Could it have something to do with aquatic insects, which are not present in the sea? Or have spinners actually been used enough in marine angling to draw the conclusion in the first place?

There is, indeed, need for much fascinating and important research.

Combining the two approaches—*imitation* with *exaggeration*—is not yet a common practice except in certain forms of angling such as chumming and trolling. Yet there is a gradually increasing awareness of the efficacy of this form of angling. Some anglers, for instance, have solved the problem of enticing large brown trout to the surface by combining a large "teaser" fly—usually a big bass bug or a streamer—with a dropper fly. They usually

present and work the combination in a manner which suggests that the larger is chasing the smaller—particularly when a streamer is used. This competitive situation stimulates the trout and it strikes one of the flies—usually the dropper unless a good streamer is used.

Even surf anglers are beginning to combine two lures—a "teaser" and another—and this is just the beginning!

Perhaps the most ingenious example we have seen of combining the imitation principle with the exaggeration approach is a Japanese trolling contraption that is used by commercial fishermen on our Pacific coast but which has only recently been introduced on our Atlantic side. This device, which has been recently modified to suit angling gear, combines a light, wood and metal planer with a number of lures of soft plastic that are remarkable imitations of a squid or octopus. One lure is leadered from the line just above the planer, and two more below. When trolled, the planer takes the

lures down at almost a 45-degree angle. On the Atlantic
coast the rig has so far been chiefly employed for bluefish, and "doubleheaders" and "tripleheaders" are common.

Another example of gross exaggeration is found in
the sets of large flasherspoons—sometimes called "cowbells" or "Christmas trees"—that are used with some
sort of bait chiefly for certain species of salmon and
trout. The upper set of one to three spinners may each
be longer than four inches and broader than one-and-
one-half inches. A foot or so below these flashers are
two to four more spinners. These are much smaller and
more round in shape. Finally, a bait of some sort—a
worm, rigged minnow, or even a single salmon egg—is
leadered a foot or so behind the last spinner. It is a
ludicrous appearing apparatus, yet very formidable for
a number of gamefishes, including landlocked salmon.

Fishes may be sensitive to colors and their exaggeration in a manner, and to a degree, that is quite
unappreciated. The color blue, for instance, while com-
monly incorporated in many lures for marine fishes, can
apparently have a most negative effect upon both saltwater and freshwater species under some circumstances.

The following statement, from an expert, is highly interesting in this regard:

"When we knew definitely we were coming to the Aquarium at Coney Island we started to experiment with color, both for the ornaments in the proposed tanks and for the tanks themselves. We also experimented with a number of new materials. Our methods of experimentation were to prepare slabs of wood and concrete, stone, coral and other solid materials, coat them with the material to be tested and put them in the tanks in which fishes were living. The fishes used were all strains of fishes which we had had for years and of whose behavior and tolerance we had a fair knowledge. Among the most suitable material we found for building tanks was fiberglass cloth and polyester resin. Colors were obtained for those and tanks were made and slabs of colored polyester resin were used, all without causing the fishes any trouble whatever.

"We used this material then, when we built a number of tanks, especially those made of plywood lined with fiberglass and coated with the polyester resin. Some of the resin was tinted white, some black and some blue, all with tints and dyes which had been previously tested without loss of fish. After several months we noticed that while the fishes living in the black and white tanks lived for a normal expectancy, fishes living in the blue tanks seemed to die earlier than we expected for no apparent reasons, although Dr. Nigrelli could always find some parasite or other in them. However, infestation was not sufficient to cause death in his opinion.

"We tried both fresh and sea water in these tanks

and had the same result with all fishes. When we scraped the blue stained resin from the tank and relined it with the same mix but with a black or white stain the tanks then gave apparently satisfactory service and the fishes lived to what we considered a normal age.

"We were never able to trace any deaths to the pigment per se, but certainly the color itself seems to be causing the difficulty." *

The use of bait, whether live or dead, also involves certain principles that can have broad application. One of these principles might be termed the "choice tidbit" approach and consists of presenting a particularly choice item of food to a fish that is not in a mood to bite. Examples of the "choice tidbit" approach can be found in the use of soft-shelled crayfish, hellgrammites (dobsons), leeches and tiny frogs for smallmouth bass; grasshoppers, caddis larvae and salmon eggs for trout; and hermit crabs and "shedder" crabs for many marine fishes. Even worms—both upland and marine—can be considered in this category.

Another principle is to combine the "choice tidbit" approach with the exaggeration approach. This principle, as we have seen, can be exemplified by chumming, or by the set of flasher spoons with some sort of choice bait bringing up the rear. Even the bait itself, in these instances, can be rigged to exaggerate. In chumming, for instance, the bait can be conspicuously larger than the items of the chum; and when flasher spoons are trolled a dead minnow can be rigged to spin far more violently than it ever would in life. But here again is a

---

* Personal communication from Dr. C. W. Coates, Director, New York Aquarium.

persistent problem in angling: just how much larger than the chum should the cut bait be? And just how fast should the minnow spin? Here, art must take over pending the answers of science, if they ever come.

It is at this point that the exceptions to the rules always become most apparent—the occasional incident that belies all theory. One encounters many of these over the years. There is the case of the neophyte angler, for instance, who was reported to have made his first surf cast, backlashed severely, yet won a tournament when a monster striped bass seized the plug while it was floating almost at the angler's feet and while he worked at the "bird's nest". And there's the case of the angler (?) who tramped down the center of the river pool with his rod over his shoulder and the bait dangling in the water some 30 feet to the rear. He is reported to have caught a seven-pound walleye.

But the event that is most indelibly etched in my mind was the case of the solitary surf angler on a beach in Florida many years ago. We report it here not because it was an "accident", but because it exemplifies how faith and patience can challenge even the latest developments in skill and science.

We first saw the solitary figure in dark clothing squatting on the beach—his crude surf rod planted in the sand —in early February. He was small in stature and his head was slightly bent over as if meditating or asleep. As we passed by him we noted that he was awake and alert so we asked him: "Any luck?" Immediately his head came up and his face was a wide grin. "Byme by," he said.

During the remainder of the month we visited this beach frequently—either to fish, or swim, or both—and almost always encountered the solitary figure in the dark clothing, squatting impassively with his crude surf rod anchored in the sand beside him. And each time we would ask him of his luck and each time the head would come up with the friendly grin and he would reply "Byme by."

February passed into March and March into April and still the man sat there, catching nothing, but always ready with his affable grin and rejoinder: "Byme by!"

It was about mid-April that it happened. We had jogged down the beach about a quarter of a mile and had entered the surf to float and dog-paddle while the gentle, warm current carried us north. Keeping a watchful lookout for the telltale "light bulbs" of the heinous Portuguese Man o' War, we sighted the figure of a surf angler in dark clothing struggling mightily with his rod. We sprinted to shore and ran up the beach just in time to witness the little man with the grin drag a big jack crevalle up from the sea. Never had we seen one as large—it must have weighed close to 30 pounds—and we expected to hear something about "byme by." But the happy little man just said "Good-bye" as he scurried up the beach dragging his catch. We never saw him again.

Just as certain basic principles can be incorporated into the design of lures, so can others be employed in the presentation of these lures. Such principles take the form of basic techniques and can be considered under well known or little known terms. The term "jigging", for instance, is known to many anglers; but it is to be doubted that such other terms as "slow lift", "slow creep", "natural drift", "dredging", "stripping", "tightening up", "climbing the rope", "leverage", etc. mean very much to most anglers. So let's consider each of these.

THE SLOW LIFT

This is basic technique used in bottom fishing for all species in fresh and salt water. A highly sensitive rod is essential for its proper execution. It consists, essentially, of raising the bait—ever, ever so slowly—from the bottom and then dropping back. It has two advantages: (1) it attracts fish to the bait, and (2) enables the angler to determine when the fish has the bait in its mouth. Sounds simple, but it requires much practice to master.

THE SLOW CREEP

This is an equally basic technique for fresh and salt water, whether used in trolling or casting. The principle here is to move the lure or bait just above the bottom— and occasionally touching it—very slowly yet with varying speed. This is a more difficult technique to master than the slow lift.

THE NATURAL DRIFT

This is the principle used in successful nymph and salmon egg fishing for trout, and in persistently successful chumming for bluefish, tuna, etc. It consists, essentially, of allowing a bait or lure to drift with the current —either at the bottom, top, or in mid-water—in a manner that is not different from an unattached food upon which the fish has become conditioned to feed.

CLIMBING THE ROPE

This refers to a fish that has seized a bait, yet does not have the hook in its mouth. The problem is to induce the creature to seize all, and here again art replaces science.

LEVERAGE

This term refers to the elbow room needed for striking or "tightening up" when a fish has seized a bait or lure. Sometimes striking is in order; at other times, tightening. But leverage is very important.

JIGGING

While the technique, or principle, of jigging is known to a multitude of anglers, there are some variations of the art that may "come handy", as our "downeaster" guides might say. Jigging is usually done vertically from an anchored boat or horizontally by trolling or casting. In either case, the appropriate action is the same—a quick upward or forward movement followed by a somewhat slower, backward movement for settling. The timing of this action and the length of stroke can be all important.

STRIPPING

This is a form of jigging while retrieving a lure with a flyrod. The line is pulled in by the hand in a series of jerks with only slight pauses. When used with streamers —particularly Marabous—the technique can be highly effective for trout and landlocked salmon.

DREDGING

This term refers to trolling a lure on the bottom, particularly in very deep water. The technique is chiefly used for lake trout during the summertime when these fish may be at depths of a hundred feet or more. Metal lines ("hardware") or leaded lines are often used with a three or four ounce sinker for sounding the bottom while combining trolling with jigging.

The preparation and hooking of baits is a very important matter for those many anglers who stoop to conquer. The most valuable feature to be sought here is rapidity of action—vibration or undulation—without spinning or rapid turnover. (An exception to this is the "spun minnow", which we shall discuss shortly). This characteristic is usually gained through flexibility which, in turn, can be produced in several ways. In preparing a whole fish for trolling, for instance, sections of the backbone can be delicately dissected out or it can be severed in a number of places without removal. In the case of eels, the task is much simpler. They can be placed in a burlap or muslin bag and swung against a hard surface a number of times. An even better method for preparing eels is to kill them and immediately pack them in salt for about an hour, rinse and put them into the refrigerator for overnight. Then wrap and freeze them for future use. They will be flexible when they have thawed out.

Cut bait for trolling should also emphasize flexibility. This can be accomplished by cutting the strip narrow and bevelling the head end. Splitting the "tail" for as much as one-third of the body length will often improve the action and also tend to keep the bait from spinning.

We might mention here that our chief objection to many commercial lures is their lack of emphasis on slenderness and rapidity of action. This is particularly true of commercial bucktail and hackle streamers: they are prone to be too bushy, the hair has often had the "life" boiled out of it, and the hair or the hackle feathers are not sufficiently parallel with the body. As for commercial Marabou streamers—these are apt to be atrocities. A single, well selected Marabou feather that is correctly tied in with the body is all that's necessary.

In the matter of the "spun minnow", we seem to be dealing with a bait that is almost singularly attractive to trout and salmon. An effective method or preparation is as follows:

1. Take a live minnow and kill it with a rap on the head.
2. Pass a snelled hook—one without an eye—through

both jaws—from lower to upper—and thread up onto the "gut". Then repeat so that a loop of "gut" is formed.

3. Now pierce the side of the minnow with the hook to the rear of the dorsal fin, then run it through and back out again on the same side.

4. Now tighten the "gut" between the jaw loop and the hook so that the posterior portion and the tail of the minnow are slightly bent. The degree of this bend will determine the rate of the spin.

The proper hooking of worms—both the garden hackle and sea varieties—is also very important. When stream fishing or stillfishing in fresh water, we almost invariably hook the worm once in the middle; when trolling fresh water, we hook the worm at the head end, thread it up onto the "gut" of the snelled hook and hook it again near the middle so that a loop is formed with a sizable portion of the worm dangling. We use this same method when trolling sea worms, but often use two or three at once.

When fishing for weakfish (sea trout, gray trout, squeteague, etc.) in a tidal current, the sea or sand worm can be hooked in the head only.

There remains one more technical area that can be of invaluable assistance to the angler. This is concerned with the ability to interpret hydrographic maps of lakes, estuaries and the sea, and the use of two or three instruments for determining temperatures. Surprisingly, this ability requires but little effort, homework and experience.

As we have mentioned, many states have surveyed their lakes for purposes of fishery management, and copies of survey maps are often either obtainable from fish and game departments or can be consulted in certain libraries. And United States Coast and Geodetic Survey charts are usually obtainable from the nearest office of that federal agency.

For the angler who wishes to "go all out" in this area, certain electronic instruments have been recently devel-

oped to satisfy this desire. Thermisters (electronic thermometers) for instance, are now available. These enable an angler quickly to determine the thermal stratification of a lake without the labor of a hand pump or a reversing thermometer. And portable, sonic depth finders are also on the market, which can be used from a rowboat or canoe.

It is now possible for many anglers to spend many pleasant evenings poring over maps, making lures, and preparing for successful safaris to strange and far-off waters.

7
The Art and the Science In Fresh Water

To shorten the time between bites. —Sportfishing Institute

The geography of the North American continent, together with strange and forbidding aspects of the sea, persuade most American and Canadian anglers to do their angling in fresh water only. Early introduction to angling in nearby lakes and streams may have taken well and the unfamiliar dimensions of the sea, or its distance away, may be discouraging. Then, of course, there is the prevalent misconception that all saltwater angling must be done with heavy rods and big hunks of lead.

An interesting result of this angling focus has been the elevation of certain freshwater gamefishes into great prominence. The smallmouth bass, for instance, becomes known as "inch for inch and pound for pound the gamiest fish that swims", and probably more words are written about angling for trout, smallmouth bass and largemouth bass than for all other species combined.

Under such circumstances it may seem presumptuous, if not a grave immodesty, to suggest techniques for catching these and other freshwater fishes. Surely the best methods must now be known and well established, and surely there is but little room for further study.

Yet this is one of the most challenging aspects of fish and fishing. Mere custom and practice are, in themselves, no guarantee of validity, and the ultimate answers on how to get fish to bite at any time and in any quantity will, we're sure, always remain under a veil of mystery. To paraphrase, "We'll never be able to fool all of the fish all of the time."

But progress can be made, and if any of the observations contained in the notes that follow serve "to shorten the time between bites" for any other angler, then they will not have been recorded in vain. So let's start with the smallmouth bass, one of the finest of gamefishes even though not "inch for inch" etc., the gamiest that swims.

THE SMALLMOUTH BASS (*Micropterus dolomieu*)

Prefers large, fairly cool lakes and rivers with large areas of stony bottom. Frequents weed beds on occasion. Begins spawning activities when water reaches about 60° F. Males prepare depressions in sand or gravel for nests, and guard these until eggs hatch. In some lakes, nests may be in as little as two feet of water, in others as much as 12 feet. Will often run up tributary streams a short distance to spawn. Fish tend to remain in spawning regions of lakes for several weeks after spawning or until second or third week of July. In many lakes—particularly when spawning regions are quite shallow—smallmouths can be taken in large numbers on popping bugs and certain other surface lures, bucktail and Marabou streamers, small jointed plugs, certain spinners and small metal spoons.

In such situations, try large, flyrod mouse of deer hair; dress well to keep it floating and just twitch it every few seconds; cast frequently and keep moving slowly. Try Nos. 0 or 1 Mepps * in brass finish with and without red and yellow bucktail; retrieve steadily. Try Woblrite in scale brass finish. Try Marabou streamers in orange or Black Ghost patterns. Try Mirrolures in "MM" and "00M" series. Try small bottom lures of head, eyes, and stubby fuzz of nylon with hook turning up and use "slow creep".

If fish are in water over five feet in depth, troll certain lures in propeller wash from 25 to 60 feet astern.

---

* Mentions of this and other brand name products in this book are made without solicitation or commercial sponsorship of any kind.

This is probably the most effective over-all method for taking smallmouths on artificial lures that has yet been discovered. Keep lures close to bottom and don't lean over gunwales of boat, or use oars or paddles. Troll at a speed of about three or four miles per hour. Try jointed Mirrolures of "00M" series in natural finishes or in brown and yellow finishes—former during overcast days and evenings and latter in bright sunlight. *Vary speed of Mirrolures ever so slightly with hand.* Try No. 0 or No. 1 Mepps in brass finish with and without red and yellow bucktail; never allow bucktail to spin: if torque is too great, try other brass spinners with the bucktail. Should have precise action and bucktail should be *sparse* and *streamlined* on a No. 5 to 7, long-shanked hook with straight eye and curved in one plane. Try Marabous in orange or Black Ghost patterns. These, too, should never spin. Keep at least one proven lure as a model and compare its appearance and action with others.

When smallmouths have moved into deeper water, trolling may be highly effective only on overcast days and during evenings. Lures may need to be weighted slightly. This applies to rivers as well as lakes. Bass can sometimes be located by trolling at mid-day in these situations (small fish may strike) and then approached by the "choice tidbit" method.

For this method use anchored boat and "slow lift" technique. Fish may be in as much as 30 feet of water. Fish bottom and just above with worms, tiny frogs, hellgrammites, soft-shelled crayfish and leeches. When fish takes bait, it usually swims very slowly. Don't strike for about ten seconds or more and then strike hard. If too soon, wait for as long as a half-minute. This seldom is necessary unless fishing with live minnows.

Fish jumps with its mouth open, so keep tension. Will dig suddenly when close to boat. (Watch this.) When fish goes under boat to other side, put rod under water to prevent fouling. Fish can be "horsed", and can often be prevented from jumping by putting rod under water. (This is not considered sportsmanlike.) Will usually regurgitate food from stomach while fighting. Tremendous willpower; strong; good staying quality; a deliberate fighter with a rather stereotyped pattern of behavior.

THE LARGEMOUTH BASS (*Micropterus salmoides*)

Unlike the smallmouth, prefers warm, weedy situations and shallow water. Spawns when water temperature is about 65° F. and guards newly hatched young for several days or until decides that they are good to eat. This disperses fry.

For most effective angling results, must be considered in three general zones: (1) northern U. S. and southern Canada, (2) central U. S. and (3) southern U.S. Fish in southern zone grow more rapidly and all year round —may reach 20 pounds—while fish in northern zone may be in old age when they reach three pounds. Central zone is in between. Bass in northern zone easiest to catch with southern zone second. Central very difficult due to heavy fishing. Tends to be a nocturnal feeder.

In northern zone, try casting with "bass bugs" and

popping plugs near lily pads or in "holes" within the lily pads any time of day or night, but particularly during evenings and after dark. Try black Jitterbug after dark and frog-pattern Jitterbug during the day. Try casting within a foot or two of shore during evenings or at night. Try different types of retrieves—from long waits to steady. Also try Mepps spinners with and without bucktail, Mirrolures and other plugs such as Dying Quiver and Lazy Ike. Try plastic ("rubber") worms with "slow creep" technique.

In central zone, with its wide variety of situations and heavy fishing pressure, large bass can become almost immune to capture. Most effective method is live bait, and even this fails to catch the nine and ten pound fish that are present in some states of this zone. Try large golden shiner or medium sized calico (crappie) hooked in the jaws and hung on a maximum of eight-pound test monofilament about three feet below a conspicuous bobber. Pay out 100 feet or more of line and troll (paddle, row or power) very slowly. When live bait begins to jump out of water, take rod in hand and wait. If fish grabs bait, allow to run, stop, and run again; then strike very hard. (P.S. You probably won't hook him.)

Southern zone is more susceptible to various methods, including "rubber worms" retrieved by the "slow creep" technique. Largest fish, however, are nearly always taken by live bait and in the manner previously described.

One of the greatest of challenge fishes: Learns quickly from experience; fights well, but not as well as the smallmouth; reaches much greater size in central and southern zones. Its weedy habitat often prevents "clean" angling.

THE LANDLOCKED SALMON *(Salmo salar)*

Prefers cold, oligotrophic lakes and has seldom been introduced outside of northeastern United States and eastern Canada. Considered by many to be the king of freshwater game fishes. Spawns in autumn in inlets and outlets of lakes; eggs are buried in redd as in the case of others members of the trout and salmon family. The landlocked salmon is a strain or subspecies of the great, sea run Atlantic salmon.

For several weeks after ice-out, and sometimes for as long as two months, landlocks can be taken at the surface on bucktails, streamers, metal, and certain types of plugs. These can be trolled or cast; latter requires considerable skill and "know how". Try red and yellow bucktails, red and yellow hackle streamers (the red outside the yellow), Marabou streamers in orange and Black Ghost patterns. Also try orange Flatfish, small pearl wobblers, Woblrite, Sidewinder, and other spoons in dull brass finish.

Troll one streamer lure just under surface about 25 feet astern in propeller wash or paddle swirls, or try streamers in tandem on each line—one about two feet in front of, and slightly below, the other on separate leaders; another set about 80 feet astern. Move up to four miles per hour, vary speed; work drop-offs of ledges and shoals, and occasionally work over shoals. Jig streamers every few seconds.

Cast over ledges and shoals and employ stripping or

uneven retrieves. Salmon will follow lure, from side to side; is a "nipper", so small tail hook usually pays off if well hidden in streamer fly. Scent seems also to be a factor, so coat streamer from time to time with slime of live minnow.

Fish is a sudden "flurry feeder", and quits just as suddenly; is lightning fast and a spectacular jumper—"gleaming like a newly minted silver dollar". Jumps with mouth shut, so relax tension on line for an instant when fish comes out of the water. After brief fight, fish swims to boat and may lie on side as if finished; don't be fooled, because things just begin at this point; will jump and shower you with water; occasionally will jump into boat. If fishing alone and close to shore, salmon can often be towed out a bit with power after first flurry, and fought under more favorable circumstances.

As lake stratifies significantly, landlocks "go down" and are difficult, if not impossible, to entice to surface. Locate depth of thermocline and troll flasher spoons such as Sebago and Dave Davis, with worm or spun minnow, near upper margin of thermocline. (Use a No. 1 to 3 hook that is snelled without eye).

A great challenge fish and fighter; an aristocrat that cannot be hurried.

THE LAKE TROUT OR TOGUE (*Salvelinus namaycush*)

Prefers very cold water and cannot survive even moderate temperatures for more than a few minutes.

This destines the species to live in the hypolimnion of oligotrophic lakes during summer. Seems to prefer about 40 to 48° F. From late autumn to perhaps midspring, fish may be at any depth and even close to shore; hence can often be taken at, or near, surface on light tackle for several weeks after ice-out. At this time try Mirrolures of the "00M" types, Woblrite and larger metal lures. In some lakes, short-shanked flies of the Edson Dark Tiger pattern with small brass spinners are effective; bucktails and Marabous may also score. Troll lures 60–90 feet astern; weight them if necessary.

During summer, lake trout must be "dredged" at depths of 50 to 150 feet. Fish is usually on or near bottom. This requires heavy line—metal or metal-filled —or very heavy sinker. (Not much sport but good meat). Best deal may be 20 or 30 pound test Monel metal line —up to 500 feet—with four-ounce sinker and saltwater or special reel for wire line. Use Harnell glass rod with pulley tip. Terminate line with three-way swivel and sinker, and run four or five-foot leader to spoon—preferably a Huntington Drone in Nos. 2 or 2½ (in strange lakes). This spoon "rides up" and will not readily foul bottom. Troll slowly, jig, and sound bottom every ten seconds or so. When fish strikes, it will fight for a few seconds and then line will be limp. Keep cranking, because fish is usually on. When line is vertical, under boat, keep on cranking. Fish will usually begin to fight again when it hits thermocline; doesn't like change in temperature. Take care here and nurse fish slowly to top.

A good, strong gamefish when caught on light tackle, but little more than "a rubber boot with fins" when dredged. (P.S. Tastes much, much better than rubber boot!)

THE BROOK TROUT (*Salvelinus fontinalis*)

Prefers cold water—usually less than 63° F. and is natively a creature of upland brooks, cold meadow streams and cold lakes. Is not nearly as well adapted to warmer, cascading streams as the rainbow trout or introduced "brown". Generations of hatchery breeding have taken wildness out of the "brookie".

In streams (wild fish), try brightly colored flies—both wet and dry—such as McGinty, Silver Doctor, Parmachene Belle, Montreal, Bee, etc. McGinty is usually sure fire; fish it dry or wet. Approach stream quietly and don't let shadow or yourself be seen. Flies can be used like bait.

Many baits are effective, from worms to grasshoppers. "Brookies" like to lurk under logs and in holes under banks. Allow bait to drift down into these situations.

In cold lakes, particularly small ones, "brookies" can usually be taken on a number of well presented lures and baits; Daredevils, Mepps, brightly colored streamers, June Bug spinners with worms, etc. These can be trolled or cast, but allow to sink into the cold layer of water.

A beautiful, vulnerable fish; a "squirmer" when hooked, and delicious eating. In northern wilderness country, often difficult to catch large ones because eagerness of small ones. (P.S. Blackflies and native "brookies" seem to go together; use face net or drench with repellent.)

THE RAINBOW TROUT (*Salmo gairdneri*)

Prefers cold lakes, and cold streams and rivers of the "cascading" types. Big adults ascend streams (from lakes) in spring to spawn; return to lakes soon afterwards. Progeny tends to remain in stream until about 10–12 inches and then descends to lake; then usually lurks in or just under thermocline during summer stratification. Must be fished here, under such circumstances, and this can be difficult.

In streams, try wet flies in gray patterns such as Gold Ribbed Hare's Ear; also gray and pale yellow patterns; also try pale yellow, or black, alone. In streamers, try Black Ghost, in Marabou, particularly during early part of season. Reduce size of fly as season progresses.

For dry flies, try light and dark Cahills, Irresistibles, Female Beaverkills, Adams, Black Gnats, and Yellow Mays; also brown or gray bivisibles. As season progresses, use smaller flies—particularly bivisibles—up to No. 20. Use 11-foot leaders tapered to 6X with latter.

Rainbows like metal and are suckers for the "choice tidbit" approach; also are attracted by certain types of small plugs. In streams, try Mepps Nos. 0 and 1 in the nickel finish, Woblrites, and Phoebes. Try Mirrolures in the "MM" and "00M" series; cast these across stream, start them with surge, and retrieve fairly rapidly.

For "choice tidbit" approach in streams, try oil-pack salmon eggs if legal; if not legal, try Velveeta cheese molded into balls the size of salmon eggs. If this is also not legal—for some strange reason the development of excellence in fishing, in our society, is prone to penalty—try grasshoppers. (As far as we know, laws have not yet been passed against grasshoppers except for "fly stretches"!)

Here's how: Present any of these as if fishing with a nymph. In other words, use a leader at least nine feet long and tapered to 3X, 4X, or even 5X. Then use a No. 10 or 12, short-shanked hook and bury it in one of the baits. The bait should be cast up and across stream and allowed to sink gradually as it is carried down by the current. (Some weight may be necessary such as BB split shot or a piece of strip lead.) When it has been allowed to go downstream about 50 feet, allow it to "hold" about ten seconds, and then retrieve it slowly for a repeat performance. Chumming will often help.

In this type of angling, a strike may seldom be felt: the line may only twitch slightly. This calls for alert and sensitive attention. A big advantage can be gained by use of Polaroid glasses; drugstore variety is a help, but custom ground jobs are a real optical instrument.

When line twitches, don't strike; just "tighten up".

In lakes during summer try sets of flasher spoons ("cowbells") trolled in, or just under thermocline, with worm, spun minnow, or salmon eggs, but be sure to check law books each year just as the baseball pros check ground rules before each game. Otherwise, pleasure can be spoiled.

In lakes during autumn—a beautiful time to angle for these fish—try small bucktail streamers—and we mean sparse and streamlined! Even try pale blue with a red tail and tinsel body. Troll or cast these at surface or just below. Also try red and pale yellow.

For a sinking fly-line, use Dacron in the size that is

suited for the rod. For a floating fly-line, use nylon in the same manner.

An exquisite game fish; lightning fast and a fine jumper. Possibly only a notch below the "Silver King" (landlocked salmon).

THE BROWN TROUT (*Salmo trutta*)

One of the most perfectly suited exotic animals ever introduced to the North American continent: The brown trout has thrived in thousands of miles of moderately warm streams—particularly in eastern United States— ever since its introduction. Much better suited for these streams than the native brook trout; (Indians never had it so good). Also, like the pheasant, it is basically a wild animal despite artificial rearing and selection.

Prefers streams and rivers in the high 60's and low 70's; also lakes that are suitable, where they will grow large and grotesquely "fat". Doesn't need these lakes, however: Will also grow huge—but usually less fat— in streams and rivers. In both situations it becomes a sulky, temperamental "cannibal". Learns quickly from experience and becomes very difficult to catch. Very few—if any—anglers are its master. Like rainbow, how- ever, has grave weakness to "choice tidbit" approach. This is unfortunate; possibly the greatest dry-fly fish in the world. In fact, many books have been written about dry-fly fishing for browns. We can add nothing except for the neophyte, in this area.

In streams, try wet flies in brown to gray patterns, such as March Brown and Gold Ribbed Hare's Ear. Try, also, a light colored fly about 18 inches behind a dark colored fly. Cast these upwards and across stream and hold tension for awhile without retrieving; then twitch as if one were chasing the other. Practice this technique, because correct presentation is the secret for catching brown trout.

Bucktails and streamers can be very effective for catching large fish. Locate "home" of large fish first, if possible, and then go to work evening after evening or morning after morning. Overcasts after the beginning of a rain are also favorable. Try small bucktail, or squirrel tail, or Marabou streamers with tinsel body and red tail. These are usually good enough. If in pool of stream with overhanging rock or bank, draw streamer past these with acceleration on the curve followed by slow, steady retrieve or rapid stripping. Do this again and again, evening after evening.

If in large pool of unknown depth, bucktail or Marabou can be weighted, paid out and jigged from head of pool, then paid out again. It is usually a matter of "byme by". These "dog-trout" as they are often called, are a "breed of their own".

Great weakness of the brown trout is its vulnerability to a well-presented worm at daybreak, a live, slimy sculpin in the darkness, or a beautifully presented nymph early during a rain. In fact, a worm can also be very effective when Nature begins to cry. Of these, the nymph is the most "sportsmanlike" approach. Cast the nymph well upstream and across and allow it to drift down with the current and tumble over the bottom. Watch for the twitch in the line and tighten. (P.S. Chances are it is bottom.)

Brown trout can also be taken in lakes by trolling a live or spun minnow in thermocline.

A great challenge fish but not a great fighter (big ones will sulk) but a "natural" for dry-fly fishing—perhaps the greatest of angling arts.

THE GREAT NORTHERN PIKE (*Esox lucius*)

A native of the Great Lakes drainage and other northern watersheds. Prefers "warm" weedy waters. Very abundant in Canada, where it was once considered a trash fish or "snake" by native guides, and something to be thrown overboard. Official gamefish status in Canada acquired only during recent years as result of American tourist attraction to big fish.

Spawns during spring in shallow water. Eggs adhere to vegetation or sink to bottom.

To catch: cast or troll Daredevils or brass spoons along margins of weed beds. If casting, allow spoon to sink and then jig during retrieve. When fish strikes, will fight initially and then give up.

A fierce creature of the north. When over five pounds, makes excellent fish chowder.

THE EASTERN CHAIN PICKEREL (*Esox niger*)

Another member of the pike family, but with more on the ball; a representative of the Atlantic coastal drainages from Canada to Florida. Also prefers weedy situations and also a fierce, "stupid" creature; but fights better than northern pike.

Try Daredevils and other wobbling spoons, including

Woblrite. Also try spinners with bucktails; also Mir-rolures in the "MM" and "00M" series. Then try Mepps in Nos. 1 and 2, with and without red and yellow bucktail. If this does not work, shift to live bait, "skitter," or go home. You've probably had it for that day.

Skittering is done with very long, old-fashioned bamboo pole with a line about 10 feet long. Hook is attached to end of long cut bait of pickerel belly. Cast into hole or pocket in weeds and give slithering, eel-like action to bait. When fish strikes, make him "climb the rope" before setting hook. After playing fish, pull in rod and line hand over hand.

An excellent "bread and butter" game fish. Fights much longer than the great northern pike and jumps often. Is usually smaller (a large one weighs three pounds and a monster is six).

THE MUSKELLUNGE (*Esox masquinongy*)

Largest member of the pike family—reaches a weight of 60 pounds or more. Also fights a bit like eastern chain pickerel—sometimes, that is. A solitary fish with apparently much territorial demand. You locate them if you wish to go to work. Weedy situations, as usual, but with more depth. This is a challenge fish.

Try the unorthodox—small lures as described for eastern chain pickerel—and troll these in the wash of a propeller about 60–80 feet astern, as well as casting, but operate for the most part along deep drop-offs that have weed beds. When the "big boy" strikes—and he usually does eventually if you've gone about it correctly—don't be disappointed. You can easily whip a 15 pounder with very light tackle. The challenge is in obtaining the strike.

As for the big, monster muskies, these are much like monster largemouths: almost immune to capture.

THE BLUEGILL SUNFISH (*Lepomis macrochirus*)

Called "brim" in the south. One of the gamiest pansters that swims, and delicious to eat. A good fly fish. Prefers warm "rich" water, spawns in guarded nest during spring and summer. Try gradually sinking flies with twitch, or Nos. 0 and 1 Mepps. If all fails, try plastic "bubble" with small piece of worm, or fly, about two or three feet below. Move this gradually after casting, with initial, quick jerks. Work in three to ten feet of water, near shore. Also try dropper-fly about 18 inches ahead of Mepps. For fly, try Royal Coachman, No. 8, with large "wing" of Impala.

THE BROWN BULLHEAD (*Ictalurus nebulosus*)

Called "horned pout" in New England; a delicious eating fish that is usually nocturnal. Forget about artificial lures, but consider the romance of a warm summer night in a pond or lake. Bait with worms, and fish bottom with the "slow lift". Fish can often be chummed with an onion bag filled with crushed mussels, chicken guts or other meat. Fish near bag. Try different spots.

THE CHANNEL CATFISH (*Ictalurus punctatus*)

One of the biggest deals in North American catfishes:

10 pounders are common. Also the handsomest of cat-fishes, with its forked tail and streamlined body. Prefers large lakes and big rivers. Recently "discovered" in the Delaware.

In lakes—such as large ones of the Great Lakes drain-age—look for moving water, such as in narrows between lakes or between islands, or between islands and main-land where water runs deep. Creature is most vulnerable at night, in Great Lakes drainage, and can be a real challenge . . .

The little rowboat with the outboard had passed through the channel between the islands on several occasions. There was a rock close to the middle of the channel and you veered around it as you went through. We had done this many times on our way to fishing grounds, and so had countless other boats. On this oc-casion, Bert, one of our two fishing companions, seemed particularly interested in the channel. "You know," he said, "the water is deep and moves here. I'll bet you can catch channel cats off this rock. Let's stop on our way back and give it a try this evening." We agreed.

We returned to the rock late in the evening, after a mediocre day with walleyes, and were relaxing with some bottles of beer that we had thoughtfully brought along. We "beached" the boat at the shallow end of the rock, waited for darkness, and baited up the fly-rods with worms.

Sure enough, we began to catch channel catfish—two pounds, three pounds, four pounds.

Then Bert hit a real one and began to worry. "You know," he observed, "I don't think I can handle this brute without some light, and certainly not without another beer."

"O.K." said Art, our other companion, "here's a beer and I'll pour a bit of gasoline on the rock and light it."

We fed Bert the beer and began to offer him encouragement when the rock exploded in flame. Art had overcompensated in the darkness. We all dove into the water and quickly pulled the boat away from the blazing rock.

It was well on the way home before anyone spoke. Finally, Bert said in a quiet voice: "I couldn't have caught him anyway. He was too damned big for the flyrod!"

What more can be said about channel cats? Jug fishing for them like snapping turtles? Other encounters in the north? Or catching them in late autumn near the condensor flows of a big generating plant in the Delaware River?

Let's just say it's a big fish, a lot of fun, and good eating.

THE YELLOW PERCH (*Perca flavescens*)

One of the most abundant of the panfishes, with a wide range of temperature tolerance and depth. Tends to be a school fish. Food preferences also vary widely with situation and time of year. Tends to chase bucktail streamers, with spinner, during spring and early summer; are "nippers", so hang small tail hook that is well hidden in hair or hackle. For baits, try "perch bugs" (dragonfly nymphs), white grubs, hellgrammites, tiny minnows, and worms. Try drifting, or slow trolling, with these behind June Bug spinner. When a perch is caught, work area over and over again. A favorite of ice fishermen; try small, live minnows.

THE WALLEYED PIKE OR WALLEYE
(Stizostedion vitreum)

Often called pickerel in Ontario; is a member of the perch family. Prefers large lakes and rivers. Tends to be a school fish and nocturnal in its feeding habits. Tends to move inshore during late evening and on overcast days, from deep water. Try slow trolling, near bottom, or off ledges or weed beds, with Mirrolures in the "00M" series, or with June.Bug spinner with worm or live minnow. Also try drifting with spinner and bait. Fish is susceptible to teasing—often in deep water up to 50 feet or more during day. When one fish is caught, work over area again and again. Casting can also be effective with lure deep. For Delaware River, try lamprey larvae behind June Bug spinner.

A favorite with ice fishermen, and one of the best eating of freshwater fishes. Not much of a fighter.

THE CISCO OR LAKE HERRING (Coregonus artedii)

Lives in cold waters of oligotrophic lakes. Will sometimes come up into warm surface layer to feed during heavy "hatches" of mayflies—usually in early summer; also in autumn, before lake "turns over", to feed upon lake shiners. Can often be taken on wetflies during former occasions, and on tiny, jigged spoons during latter. Jig spoon at 16 to 35 feet. Can be trolled in hypolimnion in summer with small spinners. Try Nos. 0 and 1 Mepps in nickel finish about 10 to 20 feet from bottom; also jig tiny spoons.

Resembles whitefish, except mouth is terminal rather than inferior, and fish are usually smaller. Unlike whitefish, seldom, if ever, present in Atlantic coastal lakes.

The Whitefish (Coregonus clupeaformis)

Lives in cold waters of oligotrophic lakes but, unlike the cisco, is a bottom fish. Can be trolled in hypolimnion, close to bottom, in summer and in the same manner as ciscos, but spinner trolled steadily seems most effective. A favorite of ice fishermen who bait ."holes" with cooked barley, rice, tiny salted or frozen minnows, etc. at depths up to 100 feet or more. Easy method to lower this bait, or chum, is to use paper bag with stone. Lower slowly to bottom and then jerk several times. Bag will break and release chum. For baiting hooks, try tiny minnows, pieces of frozen sea scallop that has been thawed, pieces of shrimp, etc. White grubs etc. may also be effective. One of the best eating of all freshwater fishes.

The Shad (Alosa sapidissima)

A marine species of the herring family that ascends rivers to spawn during spring. Is abundant on both coasts and has recently become a popular game fish in certain coastal rivers of the middle Atlantic region where it is often called "the poor man's salmon".

Can be caught by casting or trolling during spawning run, but casting in rapids below dams is top sport. Use minimum of eight-pound test line, because fish must usually be brought in against current. Spinning tackle is preferred by most shad anglers.

Lures consisting of colored beads of red, white, and yellow and strung just above a small "gold" hook are very effective. To prevent fouling on the bottom and to obtain most suitable weight—one-fourth to one-sixth ounce—tiny, haired jigs in red and white and red and yellow, with hook turned up (see illustration) are superior.

Cast up and across current and keep line tight as lure begins to arc across current in pendulum action. When directly downstream, hold for about eight seconds before retrieving and casting again. Shad usually strikes when lure is at "four or five o'clock".

A strong, tireless fighter that often jumps well. Has a weak mouth, so should be handled gently.

For trolling, use same lures, move slowly, and fish just off the bottom. Jig lure slightly from time to time.

The Carp (*Cyprinis carpio*)

A giant minnow from Asia that was once considered in the highest esteem by most peoples throughout the world, including Americans. Has since fallen in American esteem, except by minority, but has held reputation elsewhere. Cause probably due to change in eating and culinary habits and change in perspective.

Prefers warm water and soft bottom with weeds, but cannot endure "acid" water. Is prevalent in clear, clean waters of Finger Lakes and Great Lakes as well as in muddy ponds and lakes. One of the wariest and strongest of freshwater fishes. Has been called "the bonefish of fresh water". Spawns in late spring or early summer in shallows. Eggs are adhesive, and young grow rapidly.

The first step for a successful carp safari, is to select a good location. This may be a sloping shore on a river or lake that contains big carp. One can bait the ground a day or two before with canned, "whole kernel" corn if he chooses.

Two rods should be used. These can be freshwater bait casting rods or spinning rods. A line of at least eight pound test is recommended. This is to assure a good chance against "the monster", should he be encountered.

Because successful carp fishing requires complete stillness on the part of the angler, it is suggested that a portable radio be taken along. The angler can then better relax by listening to the ball game while watching his rods.

Each line should be equipped with a small "dipsy" sinker and two hooks. These should be short-shanked, strong, and about No. 4 in size. Two forked sticks— about two feet long—and a large landing net complete the equipment.

Preparing the bait, or doughball, is a ritual that takes

place the night before. A cupful of whole, stoneground cornmeal should be placed in a saucepan. Boiling water with a teaspoon of brown sugar "per cup" is then added —a small quantity at a time—and stirred into the corn-meal, while heat is on, until the meal can be readily formed. The dough is then fashioned into a ball placed in a flour bag, and pressed tight by twisting the bag. The whole business is then put into the refrigerator.

There is no need to set the alarm clock. Carp, like middle-aged anglers, feed readily during late morning hours, afternoons, and evenings.

After a leisurely breakfast you take the doughball out of the refrigerator, pack your gear and proceed to the place. Here you approach cautiously and try to see whether carp are feeding. A ripple of water or the movement of vegetation is a good sign. If there are any signs of carp, be very careful, because carp "spook" very easily.

A piece of doughball—about the size of an aggie marble—is molded around each hook in a manner that completely buries the hook. The baits are then cast lightly out onto the carp ground and the rods placed into the two forked sticks. A slight sag is left in the lines and you take up a comfortable position within an arm's reach of the rods.

Now comes the motionless wait. This may last for an hour or more while you watch for the slight twitch of the line that signifies a carp. It may be a small carp, or it may be "the monster".

At the first sign of a twitch, you sneak your hand over to the rod and get ready. Then, if the line becomes taut you strike the fish. Be prepared to see a lot of line disappear. A 20 pound carp can strip a reel if he has enough room.

8   The Art and the Science In Salt Water

In saltwater angling, the elements of certainty and uncertainty are both greatly magnified.
    —An Angler

The seas that surround us, as we have seen, are abundant in fish life: Fish are abundant in the estuaries, the bays, the coastal waters, the waters of the continental shelves and of the great ocean currents. They move about and come and go with the seasons, and at least one species is usually present at any time to attract the angler. Often there are many. Not only this, but many fish of edible size are usually ready to bite. These facts greatly enhance the angler's chances of coming home with something for the pan or oven, winter or summer.

But even as the element of certainty is magnified, so too, is the element of uncertainty. A 50 pound codfish, for example, may take it into his head to bite a bait that was designed for a much smaller fish; a 40 pound bluefin tuna may decide to strike a lure attached to a baitcasting rod; and a 30 pound striper may suddenly consume a streamer that was cast from a flyrod. This is the element of uncertainty in saltwater angling. You never know when "the monster" will strike.

Perhaps this is one reason why most saltwater anglers use far too heavy gear. They wish to rack up a big score on the abundant fish, and don't wish to be broken up if a monster should strike. Other reasons can be found in the history of saltwater angling—a sport that mushroomed in popularity during the early 'thirties'. In those days, the hordes of anglers that entrained to the ports of embarkation of commercial sportfishing boats knew little about freshwater angling—and particularly about its finer points. Freshwater rods and reels were not designed for the corrosive action of sea water, and certainly not for cranking up a fish while elbow to elbow at a crowded rail. And meat in those times, while cheap at the marketplace, couldn't compete in price with what could be boated during the many workless days. Indeed, the early traditions and customs of saltwater angling were set by the "meat hunter".

Since World War II, a veritable revolution has taken place in saltwater angling, and the development of spinning gear, monofilament line, glass rods, new reels, small craft and powerful, efficient outboard engines are but a part of this rapid change. There has also been the tremendous surge of interest in outdoor participation sports and the "do it yourself" philosophy.

Needless to say, the newness of saltwater angling is wearing off and more and more people are discovering that marine food and game fishes are not only among the sportiest of all, but also can be had on surprisingly light tackle. For example, we now see more and more anglers using six-pound test line (practically unheard of in the "old" days) for striped bass, bluefish, and bonito; and as little as ten-pound test to meet the express-train strikes and runs of 30 pound tuna and 20 pound albacore—perhaps the "gamiest" of all fishes. The secret—if that is what it can be called—is in the length of line rather than its strength and in a rod that will not take a "set" after many hours of bending.

It is in keeping with this trend, therefore, that the notes which follow do not include such species as the broadbill swordfish and the spearfishes—marlin and sailfish. These are still largely in the hands of the professional boatman and his mate or "striker" on special fishing cruisers. But we shall consider a number of marine food and game fishes that are available to the new class of anglers and what may induce these fish to bite. If our notes deal with Atlantic coast species almost exclusively, it is due to the fact that our experience and study extends more than 20 years in this area as opposed to much less time in the Pacific. The angling principles involved, however, are applicable to both coasts, even though modifications of technique may sometimes be desirable.

One such difference can be found in the technique of chumming. On the West coast, for example, chumming with live fish—usually anchovies or sardines—is practiced extensively. This is a highly effective technique in both Pacific and Atlantic waters. In the latter region, however, ground and chopped bait is usually adequate, and supplies of large quantities of live bait are not as readily available. On the other hand, chumming with live grass shrimp is extensively practiced in certain regions of the Atlantic coast.

When interpreting the notes that follow, consideration should be given to the difference between the basic principles involved, on the one hand, and the particular manner in which these principles are applied, on the other.

THE BLUEFISH (*Pomatomus saltatrix*)

Prowls the East coast of United States from Florida to Cape Cod, Massachusetts, and sparingly northward. Prefers water over 60° F. Spawns during late spring and early summer in coastal waters. Newly hatched young invade bays and estuaries and grow to length of ten inches or more during first summer of life. These are called "snappers" or "snapper blues".

Adult blues are present the year round in Florida but only during the warmer part of year much farther north; appear in middle Atlantic region during late spring and usually remain in numbers until mid-autumn. Trolling, casting, and bait fishing—with or without chumming—are effective.

When trolling with spoons, try Sparky and Hopkins lures—the former in the six to eight inch sizes—at different depths and at varying speeds up to six miles per hour; jig lures while trolling. For trolling deep try monofilament line with three or four ounce sinker, and six foot leader to lure; or use wire line to obtain desired depth. Heavy, Canadian lake trout lures in dull nickel finish, Huntington Drone and Tony Acetta spoons may also be killers; troll these at the slower speeds, with jigging.

When trolling feathered or bucktailed lures, try red and white, red and yellow, blue and white, and red and white and blue. Japanese plastic lures in squid and octopus types, with or without planer, may also be deadly; two or three trolled simultaneously with planer will often result in "doubleheaders".

Casting can be done from beach or boat. For surf fishing, try Hopkins lures about 18 inches to two feet behind red and white "teaser" lure of some type; experiment a bit with latter. Cut bait, or whole or live small fish can be used—even freshwater species such as golden shiners. Locate fish by action of birds or other anglers.

Casting from boat should be done in concentration areas such as inlet jetties. Bird action will usually reveal these. Very light tackle can be used. Try Mirrolures in the "00M" and series, Hopkins lure, metal spoons and jigs, and bucktail jigs such as Barracuda, Snookums, and Upperman Bucktails. Try the spoons and jigs with porkrind and tail hook. If blues begin to bite swivels and sever line, don't use any swivels or try black ones.

Chumming for blues can be a fine art. First important item is the chum, which should be *fresh*—either freshly ground from fresh fish and kept well refrigerated, or freshly ground from freshly frozen fish and kept in the same manner. Menhaden, or moss-bunkers, *Brevoortia tyrannis*, mixed with some sharply cut pieces of butter-fish, *Poronotus triacanthus*, and whole spearing, *Menidia menidia*, is about tops. Don't skimp on the chum (commercial fishermen never do).

Keep a quantity of whole fresh butterfish and whole frozen menhaden for cut bait. Partially thaw latter only before cutting. Butterfish should be *cut cleanly* with sharp knife into elongate pieces. Elongate pieces should be *cut cleanly* from backs of partially frozen menhaden. Cut only a few baits at a time and keep these under damp cloth or on ice. Cut more as needed. Bury hook (attached to heavy "gut" or fine wire leader about two feet long) as much as possible in bait with hook near tail end. *Do not fray the edges of the bait in any manner!*

Allow bait to drift back and sink at the same rate and in the same manner as the chum. Do this by stripping off two or three feet of line at a time. Hold for a few seconds every ten feet or so and then continue up to 70 feet. Then reel in *slowly* so as not to make bait ragged, and repeat. Ragged baits should be replaced at once. Watch slack in line and when fish strikes allow him to take slender rod tip down a bit; then tighten up.

Use same chumming method at night; a bright light does not seem to bother fish. (See Chapter 2).

Young ("snapper") bluefish can be taken by the casting and trolling of artificial lures in addition to the conventional bait methods. Try trolling very small metal lures that do not spin too rapidly; Thomas and very small Sparky are excellent. Troll in the wash of the outboard about 30 feet astern and at surface. Jig occasionally to allow lure to skip. Stop the boat when fish is hooked and, after landing fish, cast lure quickly; chances are good for catching another by this method. Then proceed with trolling.

A superb game fish that fights savagely with varied pattern: sometimes jumps and sometimes doesn't. Apparently is more angry than afraid. Because of its abundance and behavior, is usually taken on far too heavy tackle in order to run up big scores. These big scores are then often recorded in local newspapers and this, in turn, encourages even bigger scores. Too bad.

THE WEAKFISH OR SQUETEAGUE (*Cynoscion regalis*)

Also called gray sea trout and gray trout; this species should not be confused with the spotted weakfish or sea trout of our southern Atlantic coast. Prefers bay, estuaries, and inshore ocean waters; migrations described in Chapter 5.

Casting and bait fishing are most effective for capture. For casting, try southern "clothespin" type of plug, Mirrolures in the "66M" and "00M" series, and Hopkins with strip of squid or porkrind. Cast lures well up and across tide and allow to sink, then retrieve when lure is directly across tide. Speed of Mirrolures of the "00M" series should be varied slightly; the other lures should be jigged sharply during retrieve. Keep lures within two or three feet of the bottom. Red and white patterns in the "clothespin" and Mirrolure "66M" seem most effective. Will also readily strike red and yellow "pompano" plugs and haired "squids" of the Snookums and Upperman Bucktail types with strip of squid or porkrind. Can also be taken on bucktail and Marabou streamers. Try red and yellow or red and white. Drifting and jigging with above lures can also be effective.

Chumming with live grass shrimp is probably most effective method of bait fishing. Shrimp are thrown into tide a few at a time, and hook is baited with either a sea worm (sand worm) or several of the shrimp. Hook worm at head end only and strip off line two or three feet at a time. Mark distance behind boat where strike is obtained and fish at this distance. Fish strikes very savagely and hard; has weak mouth, so handle gently.

One of the hardest striking of fishes, a squirmer, and a fairly good fighter.

THE SPOTTED WEAKFISH OR SEA TROUT
(Cynoscion nebulosus)

The ranges of the northern and southern weakfish overlap from New Jersey to Georgia; but only in a very narrow range are both species equally abundant and only during short periods.

Spotted sea trout are susceptible to the angling methods described for the northern weakfish, but are perhaps more vulnerable to the casting techniques. Try attaching No. 1 Upperman Bucktail about 18 inches behind "52M" Mirrolure.

A beautiful gamefish that is often considered to be

slightly inferior in eating quality when compared with the northern species.

THE STRIPED BASS *(Roccus saxatilus)*

Getting this fish to bite is always a challenge that usually requires knowledge and experience. When not migrating in spring or autumn, tends to bite only during certain conditions of time and tide in certain situations and only when acceptable lure or bait is correctly presented. First problem is to determine striper situations and then work out other conditions and the problem of presentations. In rivers and estuaries, on the contrary, bait fishing may be simple and effective. Let's start off with bays and estuaries and then consider other areas.

Probably the best method of locating and angling for stripers in bays and estuaries is to troll sea worms or a rigged eel behind an outboard during evening or night. Hang treble hook about 18 inches behind large June Bug spinner, and loop a sea worm onto each of the three hooks so that two-thirds length of worm is trailing. Troll slowly in midwater or near bottom. For rigged eel, prepare in manner described in Chapter 5 and rig as illustrated below.

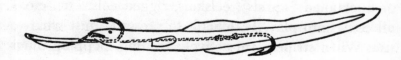

This trolling method is also effective in ocean waters, but so are some others. Try striped bass plugs—one at surface and one weighted for midwater or near bottom —60 to 150 feet behind boat during evening, night, and early morning.

Casting can be considered under two general situations: (1) surf casting from ocean beaches, and (2) casting near jetties and other rock formations, inlets, pilings, etc.

When stripers are migrating during spring and autumn—particularly the latter—they are much easier to catch by surf casting than at other times. But even during these periods, fish tend to lurk in sloughs, "pockets", patches of rocky bottom, etc. The eye needs practice for spotting these situations, and a good time for study is when the tide is near low. Look for eddying currents and other signs of bottom irregularity.

Surf casting with bait (sea worms) during spring is usually the most effective, but shedder crabs and soft-shelled crabs, which are available in late spring and summer, are among best of baits. Baits can be better held on the hook with a few windings of dark red thread, and soft-shelled crabs can be held to the hook with a hairnet.

During autumn runs of stripers, surf casting comes into its own: "popping" and "flaptail" surface plugs, underwater plugs, metal "squids" and spoons, feathered or bucktailed "squids", eelskins, rigged eels, etc., etc.— all come into play. Is difficult to prescribe just what to use. When stripers are actively feeding, popping plugs can commit mayhem; but fish can also be frequently coaxed to surface by so-called "flaptail" plug when there is no sign of feeding. The chief problem is to *find the haunts* of this fish and then *find the best time and stage of tide.* When these have been discovered, one can go to work with excited anticipation.

For casting near jetties, etc., try bucktail haired "squids" or Snookums and Upperman Bucktail types with and without porkrind. During daytime, allow to sink, and jig occasionally during retrieve; at night, use "slow creep". Correct presentation is very important.

Bait fishing from boat can be effective in bays, inlets, estuaries and tidal rivers. Chumming with live grass shrimp can make bait fishing very productive. Live bait, (including shrimp), shedder crabs and soft-shelled crabs are very effective. Whole or cut shrimp (fresh or frozen) and sea worms may also score.

A great challenge fish; strong and runs well but not a spectacular fighter; excellent eating when caught in unpolluted waters.

THE SNOOK (*Centropomus undecimalis*)

A superb gamefish of the brackish waters of Florida and the Gulf states. Often runs into adjacent fresh waters. Occasionally reaches a size of 30 pounds or more. Prefers cover such as brush, bridges, pilings, logs and mangroves. Tends to be a nocturnal feeder.

In Everglades, casting of artificial lures can be very effective; this often requires considerable skill in order to get lure under overhang. Fish seems to prefer pale yellow.

Try Mirrolures in the "52M" and "66M" series, streamers about three inches long in yellow with built-up head of black, and black body (about four long hackle feathers are needed).

Retrieve with darting action either by uneven jigging or by stripping and jigging.

Bait fishing with live shrimp among bridge pilings is popular method.

When monster snook are seen lying on the bottom like cordwood during day in inlet or elsewhere, return in late evening with live bait—preferably a "goggle eye" or other fish that will swim deep. Bait up and wait for results. They can sometimes be spectacular!

One of the greatest of all gamefishes. Fish under 15 pounds often great aerialists, although larger ones seldom jump. Delicious eating. In fact, has about everything, including a unique and mysterious challenge.

THE ATLANTIC OR COMMON BONITO (*Sarda sarda*)

Has a close relative in the Pacific bonito (*Sarda chiliensis*) of our West coast and the coastal waters of Peru and Chile. Species look remarkably alike and both are vulnerable to trolled feathered jigs, Japanese squids of plastic, spoons, etc. Mention is made of Atlantic bonito, because it can often be chummed with ground menhaden and is "gut shy". When this occurs, use a maximum of six-pound test monofilament and bury small hook completely in bait.

One of the gamiest of fishes and excellent table fare.

THE ATLANTIC BLUEFIN TUNA (*Thunnus thynnus*)

The same species as in the Pacific, but Atlantic bluefins grow much larger and behave differently. Our remarks will be confined to "school fish" up to 100 pounds.

Can be trolled, jigged, and occasionally chummed. When trolling, try feathered "squids" and Japanese plastic "squids" in the wash and outside the wash from outriggers. In the wash, try a short line (about 20 to 30 feet) with lure just under surface and in "boil", and another, longer line (up to 80 feet) in "slot" between "boil" and streak of foam. Outriggers can troll surface and a bit below in still water.

If this fails, slow down a bit and take out inner lines; replace one with cedar "squid". Then drop back a Hopkins lure or Huntington Drone spoon or heavy Canadian lake trout lure on steel or Monel metal line—preferably the latter. Permit lure to sink about 30 feet and jig with variation while trolling at speed of about three or four miles per hour. Vary speed, once in a while, to give other lures a chance.

If tuna are obviously feeding near surface—and this doesn't mean playing at surface like porpoise—try to determine target and try to match same.

School tuna can sometimes be chummed with ground menhaden. When this happens, mix cut fish liberally with chum, with occasional whole fish. For bait, try whole butterfish, cleanly cut pieces of butterfish, balls of ground chum, or pieces of cleanly cut menhaden. Allow these to drift back and sink *in precisely the same manner as the chum and with as inconspicuous a leader or line as possible.* If bait sinks too rapidly, put small pieces of split cork on line about five feet above bait. Pay out gently by stripping line from reel, or with hands from previously stripped coil. Pay out as much as 150 feet before retrieving and starting all over again.

For balls of chum, try double or treble hooks with

hank of thread for wrapping. Double hooks are easier to handle. Replace chum ball frequently.

Possibly the gamiest fish that swims, along with albacore and bonito. Extremely fast and strong, but with no aerial acrobatics. Keeps fighting until death invades cells of body.

THE LITTLE TUNA OR FALSE ALBACORE
(*Euthynnus alletteratus*)

An Atlantic tuna that reaches a weight of about 20 pounds and which is fairly common along our Atlantic coast. Invades the middle Atlantic region in late summer and autumn—often in large numbers. Is susceptible to trolling and chumming, but is highly underestimated by the average angler, probably because he doesn't realize that it is a species of tuna and just as good eating as the bluefin.

When trolling, use methods described for bluefin tuna, but also try some modifications: Try large bucktail streamers in red and yellow up to 150 feet astern and at slower speed. Also try cedar plugs at varying speeds and distances.

Many anglers consider this fish to be "inch for inch and pound for pound" truly the gamiest fish that swims. It is most unfortunate that its eating qualities are but little known. (See following chapter.)

THE FLUKE OR SUMMER FLOUNDER
(*Paralichthys dentatus*)

An abundant species in the middle Atlantic states. Has close relatives in the southern fluke *Paralichthys lethostigma,* the Gulf fluke, *P. albigutta,* the California "halibut", *P. californicus,* and the lenguada of Chile and Peru, *P. chiliensis.* Movements and migrations have been described in Chapter 5.

Drifting with live or cut bait is popular method in middle Atlantic region, although slow trolling with cut bait—particularly when tide is not swift—is usually more effective. Strips of cut bait four to ten inches in length from white or dark side of fluke (try both) with split tail and prepared in the manner described in Chapter 6 are very effective. Hook these at anterior end only, about 18 inches behind small June Bug spinner. An orange or red bead at head of spinner may increase effectiveness. Experiments with large tandem spinners have failed to show any superiority and are clumsy. Never allow bait to spin and keep it within a foot of bottom. Jig bait slightly every ten seconds or so.

When fluke strikes, wait until he "climbs rope" before striking. This requires much practice and is still a tantalizing affair.

Casting with bait or lures can also be effective. Try clothespin and pompano type plugs, or Mirrolures in the "52M" series. Red and white or red and yellow seem to be the most effective. Allow these to sink and jig them along bottom during retrieve. With bait, use "slow creep".

THE WINTER FLOUNDER
(Pseudopleuronectes americanus)

A great favorite of rowboat anglers of middle and north Atlantic coast during spring and autumn when it is abundant in bays and estuaries. Seasonal movements and spawning habits have been described in Chapter 5.

For fishing locations, try the margins of channels— particularly in tidal eddies formed by islands etc. If first spot doesn't produce after 15 minutes, pull anchor and try another. Use two flounder hooks separated by a spreader decorated with orange beads. Fish will bite pieces of sea worms (sand worms), blood worms, soft-shelled clams, hard clams, etc. Many experiments in many localities have indicated that sea worms are almost always preferred, but that the other baits will be taken readily when no choice. Use "slow lift" technique.

To shorten the time between bites, use onion or orange bag containing freshly crushed mussels or clams and large stone. Lower this to bottom and shake occasionally. Also fasten a "plumber's helper" to long pole and churn bottom from time to time. Flounders are attracted to both and seem unafraid. Every 15 minutes or so, raise chum bag, crush mollusks again with foot, and lower once more.

THE TAUTOG OR BLACKFISH (*Tautoga onitis*)

A family relative of the California sheepshead and the pejeperro of Chile and Peru. Prefers mussel beds and rocky regions where it will work its way into caverns, sometimes on its side. Shores of New England are tops for this strong species, where 12-pounders are common. Seems to be completely without "gut shyness" and strictly a bait fish.

Use small, strong hooks and work "spots" in the bottom where sinker goes a little deeper. Use "slow lift" technique and allow for just a bit of "rope climbing" before striking.

Probably best bait of all is hermit crabs, although a half or quarter of green crab or a clump of shrimp or a mussel or a section of sea clam may also score well. Can usually be readily chummed with live grass shrimp.

MISCELLANEOUS BOTTOM SPECIES

These include just about all other bottom dwelling families or "deep sea" species that are readily available to the angler—the grunts, porgies, sea basses, snappers, codfishes, rockfishes, etc. The three chief angling principles to be remembered with these fishes are (1) the "slow lift" or "slow creep", (2) possible "gut shyness" and (3) the "choice tidbit" approach. Little else is needed unless one wishes to do it the hard way.

And as for the choicest tidbit?

Well, the hermit crab certainly deserves consideration!

9

Let's Eat!

Better a sprat than no fish at all.   —Aesop

It may seem strange that in certain highly civilized parts of the world, any use of ice with fish is frowned upon by many consumers. This disfavor, however, is nothing new. The ancient and highly civilized Greeks, who prized fish as a great culinary delicacy, even prohibited the use of fresh water on fish, and their attitude was well founded.

The concern is involved with the true freshness of the fish or, more accurately, the shortness of time between the removal from the water and the offering for sale. In our country, for instance, the product offered as "fresh fish" may have been in crushed ice for several weeks or, perhaps, have been frozen for months, thawed, and kept on ice for another week or so. This does not render the product unsafe to eat. It simply permits the "aging" process, so desirable for red meat, to take place in fish. And tenderized fish is far inferior to firm, fresh fish.

Lest anyone question the accuracy of this account, what did the "fresh mackerel" you saw at the store last time look like? Was it gleaming iridescent silver with solid black lines in deep rich green? Were the eyes bright and the gills blood red? The flesh firm? Was there only a slight fishy odor? We doubt it. And this is why the ancient Greeks objected to glazing with fresh water and why many moderns suspect aging when a fish is on ice. In short, that which can be of invaluable aid in preserving the freshness of fish (chilling) is prone to be commercially abused.

We mention all this here, because we have long suspected that many anglers who are not interested in eating the fish they catch are suffering from psychological scars gained from an early introduction to the average "fresh fish" at the American marketplace. It is to be lamented.

Outside on the stone terrace of the old New England cottage, the gasoline stove breathed mightily to heat the big pot of fresh sea water with its clumps of floating rockweed. Faint rustles in the giant paper bag next to the stove were comforting assurance that the lobsters were still alive.

In the kitchen next to the terrace there was great activity. Some of the guests were stripping the newly picked corn while others were rinsing the soft clams. Next to the stove and ready to go into the pan was a heap of freshly cleaned snapper bluefish that had been caught that morning. The hostess was putting garden fresh lettuce, red ripe tomatoes and sliced cucumbers into a wooden salad bowl before adding the chilled meat of freshly cooked blue crabs. The host was mixing highballs, checking the lobster kettle, and making sure that the vintage Sauterne was chilling correctly.

As the twilight descended upon the blue waters of
the nearby estuary, all was ready—the steaming hot lobsters, the melted butter with a touch of garlic, the corn,
the crabmeat salad, the clams with cups of hot broth,
the ice cold Sauterne, and the snapper bluefish fried to
a golden brown.

All ate and drank their fill save one guest who had
had distasteful exposures to "fresh fish" early in life.
Being a gentleman, sportsman and fine angler, however,
he ate his hamburgers, corn, and salad (minus crabmeat), with zest and a sense of genuine good will towards his fellow man.

Pending a much needed betterment and grading of
fishery products at the marketplace, the angler can use
his enviable position of quality control to great advantage. Absent, for example, is the need for any "doctor-

ing" with strong sauces and poaches, and the true flavor goodness can be carefully guarded.

One of the most important characteristics of fishes that has to do with their eating quality is their tendency to take on the flavor of their environment. This accounts for the "muddy" or algae taste of some fish from warm, weedy ponds and also accounts for the "oily" taste of fish taken from harbor waters or from polluted rivers. These flavors do not affect "safeness" for eating, but they can be very distasteful.

Another factor that affects the flavor of fishes is the chief foods that they feed upon. Hatchery reared trout, for example, are inferior to wild trout; and rainbow and lake trout that have been feeding heavily upon alewife herring ("sawbellies") are inferior in flavor to trout that have been feeding chiefly upon other aquatic life.

The color of many fishes, and particularly members of the trout family, is also affected by their diet. The bright external colors of certain trout, for instance, or the yellowish or orange pink of their flesh and eggs is due to a pigment that occurs in the "shells" of insects. It is the same pigment that makes lobsters, shrimp, etc., turn red when they are boiled.

TREATMENT IMMEDIATELY AFTER CAPTURE

The first problem in quality control is what to do with the fish immediately after it is caught. The ideal procedure, of course, would be to bury it in crushed ice, but this is usually impossible or impractical. Indeed there are so many types of situations that no hard and fast rule can be recommended.

When fishing a stream, we greatly prefer the cloth and mesh creel to the old-fashioned basket. We simply drop the fish into the crcel and allow evaporation to aid in keeping the fish cool. From time to time we quickly dip the mesh part of the creel with the fish into the stream in order to aid the desired evaporation. We have learned that among the worst things we can do is to bury the fish in ferns or partially clean it.

When on a boat, and when a special fish box with ice is not available, we prefer a coarse-meshed bag such as an onion or orange bag, or a fruit basket, or the special wire basket used by commercial fishermen. This is again to allow for evaporation. With certain oily fish, such as mackerel and bluefish, ice is almost a "must".

The gutting or partial cleaning of a fish may do more harm than good. Most gamefishes, for instance, in contrast to most game mammals, are highly predaceous and have short intestines. And the food they consume doesn't quickly "ferment" and cause bloating as is the case with a deer or a rabbit. On the other hand, the digestive juices of a fish, the contents of its kidneys, and its partially digested food should not be allowed to spill onto the muscle flesh without early and thorough washing. It's almost always best to leave the internal organs of a fish, including its gills, strictly alone and intact until a thorough job can be done.

PREPARATION FOR COOKING OR FREEZING

After much trial and error, we have come to the conclusion that the preparation of fish both for cooking or freezing should be done in exactly the same manner—minus, of course, the packaging for the deep freeze. In other words, the fish that comes out of the package and is thawed should not require any further cutting. This brings up our first problem of personal preference (there will be many more) which might be entitled: *To Skin or Not to Skin.*

Possibly no angler—whether a Democrat or a Republican—would ever strongly oppose the skinning of eels or catfish. Indeed it is questionable whether any objection would be extended to the skinning of tautog (blackfish). But here agreement probably ends and we are in trouble. Some persons, for instance, insist upon skinning yellow and white perch, bluegills, walleyed pike, cod, flounders, etc., while others wouldn't even dream of such a "desecration"! Needless to say, we have no desire to enter this controversy, even though we happen to belong to the "not to skin" school of thought.

The point we should like to make here, however, is that it's much easier to skin or scale a fish shortly after it has been removed from the water than later on, and particularly before freezing. This brings us to the next problem, which might be entitled: *To Fillet or Not to Fillet.*

Here again is a matter of preference, depending upon the most desirable product for the table. The size of the fish is also a factor. One would hesitate, for example, to fillet a yellow perch, a small brookie, a sailor's choice, a bluegill, or a snapper blue. These call for whole frying. But fillets of larger fish—for broiling, frying, poaching, baking, or chowder—are often called for, and if filleting is to be done, then "'twere well it were done quickly".

Fʀᴇᴇᴢɪɴɢ

Correct packaging and quick freezing are the secrets
of quality control in storing fish in the deep freeze. First
of all, however, be sure that all traces of kidney, heart,
liver, gills, etc. are removed. The kidney, which lies just
beneath the backbone, is sometimes difficult to clean
out thoroughly because of pockets between bones. Use
the tip of the knife for this.

After rinsing the fish in cold water it can be double-
wrapped tightly in aluminum foil and freezer tape. Another excellent method, and one that we prefer, is to use
regular plastic vegetable bags and cardboard boxes
(quart size) and freeze the fish in water. The plastic
bag is packed while standing in the box, enough cold
water is added to cover, the air is sucked out of the bag,
and the bag sealed with a rubber band.

When placing the packages in the freezer compart-
ment of the deep-freeze, be sure to allow space for air
to circulate around each package. In other words, don't
pile them into a solid heap until after they are thoroughly frozen.

Oily fish such as mackerel, bluefish, and trout do not
maintain their flavor as long as the non-oily species, and
it may be preferable to use the former within a three
month period.

Cooᴋɪɴɢ

This is the most controversial subject of them all due
to the wide variety of tastes among people. In the simple
matter of frying, for instance, some persons prefer but-

ter, others prefer bacon fat, while still others insist upon the fat of salt pork. (P.S. We use corn oil.) The nature of the dip would appear to be equally controversial: white flour, cracker meal, bread crumbs or cornmeal. And as for cornmeal, some prefer the regular yellow while others will use nothing but the whole, stone ground product. (On this one we dare not comment.)

But for shallow pan frying we do have the temerity to suggest a fairly hot fire, a very light sprinkling of onion salt or onion powder, and some fresh lemons.

As for deep or so-called "french" frying—surely a misnomer—a law should certainly be passed against it. In fact we know of no more horrible custom than the American one of putting even aged fish to such a final insult. And, as if this were not enough, injury is added to insult in the form of a pasty thick batter.

But, seriously, deep frying can produce a magnificent product in the form of "fish 'n chips" if it is done correctly; so let's venture our first recipe on this one. Many fish can be used—cod, haddock, walleyes, great northern pike, etc. Here are the ingredients, and the amounts should depend upon the number and characteristics of the consumers:

1. Potatoes (Idaho or Green Mountain variities preferred)
2. Thick, skinned fillets of fish
3. Fresh eggs
4. White flour
5. Salt, onion salt, and pepper.

Cut fish into chunks about the size of walnuts, and cut peeled potatoes into pieces about two or three

inches long and one-half inch thick. Put flour, salt, and
some onion salt into paper bag. Break an egg or two
into dish, add one tablespoon of cold water per egg and
beat into uniformity.

Heat saucepan of corn or cottonseed oil, with wire
basket ready, until the oil begins to smoke slightly.
(Drop in a potato chip and see whether it will cook in
20 seconds.)

Dip the chunks of fish into the egg and water mix,
put into paper bag with flour, etc. and shake. Then
place two layers of fish chunks into basket and lower
into hot oil. (If oil threatens to boil over, lift out every
few seconds until this threat ceases.)

When fish is cooked to light brown, place on pan in
warm oven and cook second batch. Then fry the potatoes and place these on flat paper bag or paper towel-
ling and sprinkle with salt. (P.S. A tossed salad and a
chilled Rhine wine go nicely with this.)

FISH CHOWDER

Now that we have broken the ice on a very simple,
but delicious dish, let's try another. This one is tradi-
tional to America, despite our use of some modern
products. In other words, this is our version of New
England fish chowder. The ingredients:

1. Some white onions
2. Some potatoes (Green Mountain or Idaho
    preferred)
3. Some fillets of fish (white perch, yellow
    perch, smallmouth bass, walleye, north-
    ern pike, cod, haddock, tautog, etc.)

4. Evaporated milk (cans)
5. Salt, pepper, etc.
6. Butter

Peel and cut potatoes into half-inch cubes and slice one onion for every two potatoes.

If open pot is used, cover onions and potatoes with water and boil for ten minutes without lid before adding fish. Boil another ten minutes with the fish, then add evaporated milk, salt and pepper as desired. Also add big lump of butter. Simmer, then serve.

If pressure pot is used, cook potatoes, fish and onions all together for about three minutes. Then add milk and butter, simmer and serve. Sprinkling paprika well over surface, before serving, may be desired.

BROILED FISH

Broiling can be done alone or combined with baking. It also can be combined with poaching; and this is where matters can become very complicated. Broiling in the strict sense, of course, means cooking either under or over a direct open flame or other heat. In other words there is no intermediate agency of heat transfer.

Quite frankly, we have long since given up on the pure broiling of fish except for fresh swordfish steaks over charcoal. We almost always combine broiling with baking, and often with a bit of poaching. Rather than go into laborious details here, let's just offer a recipe for "broiled bonito". Ingredients:

1. Split bonito or "boneless" fillets
2. Butter and vegetable oil

3. Salt, onion salt, pepper and fresh milk
4. Fresh lemon
5. Chopped parsley and paprika

Place bonito—skin side down—in oiled broiling pan, brush with oil and dot with butter. Sprinkle lightly with onion salt and pepper, and sprinkle more heavily with salt. Place about six inches under broiler flame or electric unit and partially close oven door—about three-fourths of way. When fish begins to turn slightly brown, pour milk or court-bouillon over fish to a depth of about one-quarter inch in pan, close oven door and set to 350 degree temperature. Baste every few minutes. Add juice of lemon shortly before fish is cooked and keep basting. Turn back to broil—or return fish to broiler—during last moment if crispy brown is desired. Pour juices from pan over fish, sprinkle with chopped parsley and paprika, and serve with fresh lemon wedge.

This recipe, needless to say, is also applicable to mackerel, bluefish, "finnan haddy", trout, salmon and almost any other fish. We prefer it, however, only with the "oily" and smoked fishes. With others, we usually eliminate the poaching.

ROASTED FISH

Here is a real challenge. A six pound bluefish, lake trout, striped bass or walleye, stuffed correctly and roasted to the correct shade of brown is as much a triumph as a successfully roasted suckling pig or ribs of beef. Here is what we suggest:

1. Put fresh or freshly thawed fish (with head and tail intact, of course) upon table and estimate amount of stuffing needed to fill body cavity without bulging unnaturally.
2. Pour out packaged stuffing of choice into bowl in the estimated amount.
3. Peel and chop one large onion and add to stuffing, and moisten to desired degree with orange juice.
4. Stuff fish and sew up with needle and thread. Sprinkle with salt, pepper, and onion salt.
5. Place in greased roasting pan and place in hot oven (450 degrees) without lid. Pour on a cup of vegetable oil.
6. When skin is seared, reduce temperature to 400° and begin to baste every ten minutes.
7. Pour two cups of white dry wine over fish, when skin begins to turn brown, and reduce temperature to 350°. Maintain this and keep basting.
8. Squeeze juice of two lemons over fish at three-quarter mark and keep basting. Sprinkle with onion salt.

Serve whole on platter with parsley and lemon wedges.

Ice cold Reisling, Moselle or dry Sauterne go very well with this dish. Also summer squash, tossed salad, wax beans and fresh corn-on-cob.

POACHED FISH

We've already partially gotten into this subject with the milk and court-bouillon. Court-bouillon, incidentally, is very simple to prepare. Just cut a bunch of carrots, a head of celery and some onions and drop these into enough boiling water with some salt, peppercorns and bay leaves. Simmer for a day or so and then strain off the "court-bouillon".

Milk, as we have seen, is also a poaching agent, and so is white wine. We prefer to use the latter only with "oily" fish and here's a method. The ingredients:

1. Fish fillets
2. White wine (dry)
3. White onion or chives
4. Salt and pepper

Soak fish in enough wine to cover for about a half-hour and with some finely chopped onion. Place in poaching pan and bake in oven (350°) for about another half hour. Serve. (P.S. We're sure you may not like it.)

STEAMED FISH

This approach is rather special. It is often used by those who prefer a bland fish flavor. Here is a recipe for steamed cod with egg sauce.

1. Take a whole, or section, of cod and steam for about ten minutes per pound. (Sprinkle lightly with onion salt, salt and pepper beforehand.)

2. Prepare white sauce and add an abundance
   of finely chopped, hardboiled eggs with
   a sprinkle of paprika and chopped parsley. (P.S. The same thing can be done
   with a skinned tautog.)

Steamed or boiled fish is also delicious for use when chilled. This is one of the "lost tastes" of North America and one that should surely be revived. We had to travel a long way, for instance, to discover that steamed and chilled mullet was a delicacy. And when we encountered Congrio colorado in Chile, our mind and taste were truly stimulated.

Perhaps this is why we appreciated carp in aspic when we returned to the homeland. Here is a method:

1. Scale freshly caught carp, clean and remove gills.
2. Cut into sections, with head intact, salt
   lightly, and put into refrigerator overnight.
3. Next day, place all in saucepan and cover
   with water; add a finely chopped onion,
   bring to a boil but simmer for a half hour.
4. Remove from stove and place in refrigerator for overnight without pouring out the
   broth.

Next day you will find a delicious fish "in aspic"— with excellent flavor and texture. (P.S. Some beer and crackers go very well with this dish!)

Barbecued Fish

Barbecued fish is a delicious product but involves certain difficulties in the cooking. The chief difficulty is the strong tendency for the skin of the fish to stick to the grill. Even liberal and repeated applications of shortening may not solve the problem. Another stumbling-block is the tendency of many fishes to fall off skewers while cooking. Wooden sticks seem superior to metal, and, if an outdoor grill is equipped with a rotating skewer, a wrapping of fine wire will often help. Some fish, such as swordfish steaks, offer no problem.

Canning Fish

The home canning of certain fishes is a rather simple procedure that yields a product of superb quality. The species include ocean bonito (called "skipjack" on the West coast and "watermelon" bonito on the Atlantic seaboard), bluefin tuna, yellowfin tuna, albacore, and the little tuna or false albacore of our Atlantic coast. The last named species incidentally, while having slightly darker flesh than the others, yields a product that is every bit as good.

Actually, the commercial emphasis on "light" meat, "white" meat, etc. is very misleading. For the dark meat or "streak", which is present in the sides of all tuna and tuna-like fishes is always carefully removed before canning.

The equipment and ingredients needed for nine pints or 18 half-pints of the canned product are as follows:

A pressure cooker of the home-canning type.

Nine pint or 18 half-pint Mason jars with self-
sealing lids.

A stout knife, well sharpened.

Approximately 25 pounds of whole fish.

Five pounds of salt.

A pint of vegetable oil such as cottonseed, soy-
bean, "salad" oil, etc. (The use of oil is op-
tional, but is greatly preferred by many.)

Skin and fillet the fish as soon as possible after being caught. If it is not possible to can it within two days, wrap the fillets and place them in the deep-freeze.

Prepare a brine of one cup of salt per gallon of cold water, add some pieces of ice and soak fillets for at least four hours; overnight if more convenient. Then rinse thoroughly in running water and remove "dark streak". With false albacore this is facilitated by dipping fillets in scalding water for a few minutes so that the dark streak will become more conspicuous. Trim off meat of belly wall, rather liberally, because this is quite fat and of inferior quality.

Cut large pieces of fish from the fillets—as large as can be conveniently fitted into the jars—and pack firmly. Smaller pieces are used to fill spaces after the first two or three large pieces have been put into the jar. Pack the jars tightly to within about three-fourths inch of the top, *but no more,* and then add one level teaspoon of salt per pint jar.

If oil is to be used, enough should be added to fill any spaces within the pack and just to cover the fish. In order to allow the oil to run into the spaces, an ordinary table knife can be inserted between the glass jar and the fish, and manipulated until the spaces are filled.

Before capping the jars, make sure that their sealing edges are not chipped and then wipe these edges with a cloth so that they are clean and smooth. Dip the metal cap into hot water for about ten seconds—or keep some in hot water until used—and place it on top of the jar. Then, keeping the cap in position, screw down the metal band. Tighten firmly, but avoid "heavy persuasion". *No further tightening is necessary at any time!*

The jars should then be placed into the cooker according to the manufacturer's directions. Process them for 100 minutes at a pressure of ten pounds. (The hundred minutes are counted from the time the ten pounds of pressure has been reached.)

When this cooking period is over and the pressure cooker has been cooled and exhausted in accordance with the manufacturer's directions, carefully remove the jars and place them, right side up, on folded towels or newspapers. *Don't place them on hard, cold surfaces, and don't tighten the lids any further!*

When the jars have cooled completely, they should be tested for "seal" by tapping the lids lightly with the handle of a table fork or spoon. If sealed, the lid will have a musical or ringing tone rather than a thud or dead sound, and the jars may be put away for storage. If in doubt about any jar, put this in the refrigerator and use within a week or so.

In fact it is always desirable to have one jar fail to seal. Because this prompts an early tasting of the effort and an opportunity to decide whether or not it is superior to the "boughten" product.

Needless to say, there is much more to cooking fish than we have mentioned here. There is the matter of herbs, for instance, and the blending of different fishes into one recipe. And there is the matter of exotic sauces, etc. But it is our position that when truly fresh fish are involved, it is a question of how to let the fish speak for itself—in flavor and texture—amidst other fresh surroundings and refreshed memories. Only the wine need be old.

Index

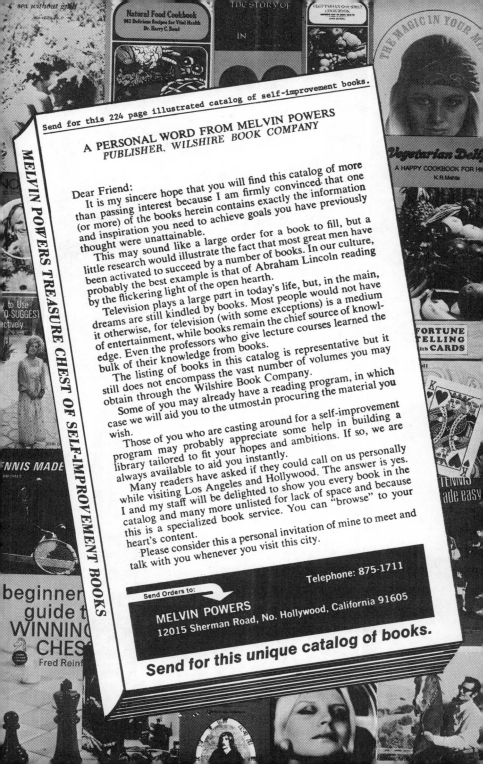

MELVIN POWERS SELF-IMPROVEMENT LIBRARY

ASTROLOGY

_____ASTROLOGY: A FASCINATING HISTORY *P. Naylor*	2.00
_____ASTROLOGY: HOW TO CHART YOUR HOROSCOPE *Max Heindel*	2.00
_____ASTROLOGY: YOUR PERSONAL SUN-SIGN GUIDE *Beatrice Ryder*	2.00
_____ASTROLOGY FOR EVERYDAY LIVING *Janet Harris*	2.00
_____ASTROLOGY GUIDE TO GOOD HEALTH *Alexandra Kayhle*	2.00
_____ASTROLOGY MADE EASY *Astarte*	2.00
_____ASTROLOGY MADE PRACTICAL *Alexandra Kayhle*	2.00
_____ASTROLOGY, ROMANCE, YOU AND THE STARS *Anthony Norvell*	2.00
_____MY WORLD OF ASTROLOGY *Sydney Omarr*	3.00
_____THOUGHT DIAL *Sydney Omarr*	2.00
_____ZODIAC REVEALED *Rupert Gleadow*	2.00

BRIDGE & POKER

_____BRIDGE BIDDING MADE EASY *Edwin Kantar*	5.00
_____BRIDGE CONVENTIONS *Edwin Kantar*	4.00
_____HOW TO IMPROVE YOUR BRIDGE *Alfred Sheinwold*	2.00
_____HOW TO WIN AT POKER *Terence Reese & Anthony T. Watkins*	2.00

BUSINESS, STUDY & REFERENCE

_____CONVERSATION MADE EASY *Elliot Russell*	2.00
_____EXAM SECRET *Dennis B. Jackson*	2.00
_____HOW TO BE A COMEDIAN FOR FUN & PROFIT *King & Laufer*	2.00
_____HOW TO DEVELOP A BETTER SPEAKING VOICE *M. Hellier*	2.00
_____HOW TO MAKE A FORTUNE IN REAL ESTATE *Albert Winnikoff*	3.00
_____HOW TO MAKE MONEY IN REAL ESTATE *Stanley L. McMichael*	2.00
_____INCREASE YOUR LEARNING POWER *Geoffrey A. Dudley*	2.00
_____MAGIC OF NUMBERS *Robert Tocquet*	2.00
_____PRACTICAL GUIDE TO BETTER CONCENTRATION *Melvin Powers*	2.00
_____PRACTICAL GUIDE TO PUBLIC SPEAKING *Maurice Forley*	2.00
_____7 DAYS TO FASTER READING *William S. Schaill*	2.00
_____STUDENT'S GUIDE TO BETTER GRADES *J. A. Rickard*	2.00
_____STUDENT'S GUIDE TO EFFICIENT STUDY *D. E. James*	1.00
_____TEST YOURSELF — Find Your Hidden Talent *Jack Shafer*	2.00
_____YOUR WILL & WHAT TO DO ABOUT IT *Attorney Samuel G. Kling*	2.00

CHESS & CHECKERS

_____BEGINNER'S GUIDE TO WINNING CHESS *Fred Reinfeld*	2.00
_____BETTER CHESS — How to Play *Fred Reinfeld*	2.00
_____CHECKERS MADE EASY *Tom Wiswell*	2.00
_____CHESS IN TEN EASY LESSONS *Larry Evans*	2.00
_____CHESS MADE EASY *Milton L. Hanauer*	2.00
_____CHESS MASTERY — A New Approach *Fred Reinfeld*	2.00
_____CHESS PROBLEMS FOR BEGINNERS *edited by Fred Reinfeld*	2.00
_____CHESS SECRETS REVEALED *Fred Reinfeld*	2.00
_____CHESS STRATEGY — An Expert's Guide *Fred Reinfeld*	2.00
_____CHESS TACTICS FOR BEGINNERS *edited by Fred Reinfeld*	2.00
_____CHESS THEORY & PRACTICE *Morry & Mitchell*	2.00
_____HOW TO WIN AT CHECKERS *Fred Reinfeld*	2.00
_____1001 BRILLIANT WAYS TO CHECKMATE *Fred Reinfeld*	2.00
_____1001 WINNING CHESS SACRIFICES & COMBINATIONS *Fred Reinfeld*	2.00

COOKERY & HERBS

_____CULPEPER'S HERBAL REMEDIES *Dr. Nicholas Culpeper*	2.00
_____FAST GOURMET COOKBOOK *Poppy Cannon*	2.50
_____HEALING POWER OF HERBS *May Bethel*	2.00
_____HERB HANDBOOK *Dawn MacLeod*	2.00
_____HERBS FOR COOKING AND HEALING *Dr. Donald Law*	2.00
_____HERBS FOR HEALTH How to Grow & Use Them *Louise Evans Doole*	2.00
_____HOME GARDEN COOKBOOK Delicious Natural Food Recipes *Ken Kraft*	3.00

_____NATURAL FOOD COOKBOOK *Dr. Harry C. Bond* 2.00
_____NATURE'S MEDICINES *Richard Lucas* 2.00
_____VEGETABLE GARDENING FOR BEGINNERS *Hugh Wiberg* 2.00
_____VEGETABLES FOR TODAY'S GARDENS *R. Milton Carleton* 2.00
_____VEGETARIAN COOKERY *Janet Walker* 2.00
_____VEGETARIAN COOKING MADE EASY & DELECTABLE *Veronica Vezza* 2.00
_____VEGETARIAN DELIGHTS — A Happy Cookbook for Health *K. R. Mehta* 2.00
_____VEGETARIAN GOURMET COOKBOOK *Joyce McKinnel* 2.00

HEALTH

_____DR. LINDNER'S SPECIAL WEIGHT CONTROL METHOD 1.00
_____GAYELORD HAUSER'S NEW GUIDE TO INTELLIGENT REDUCING 3.00
_____HELP YOURSELF TO BETTER SIGHT *Margaret Darst Corbett* 2.00
_____HOW TO IMPROVE YOUR VISION *Dr. Robert A. Kraskin* 2.00
_____HOW TO SLEEP WITHOUT PILLS *Dr. David F. Tracy* 1.00
_____HOW YOU CAN STOP SMOKING PERMANENTLY *Ernest Caldwell* 2.00
_____LSD — THE AGE OF MIND *Bernard Roseman* 2.00
_____MIND OVER PLATTER *Peter G. Lindner, M.D.* 2.00
_____NEW CARBOHYDRATE DIET COUNTER *Patti Lopez-Pereira* 1.00
_____PEYOTE STORY *Bernard Roseman* 2.00
_____PSYCHEDELIC ECSTASY *William Marshall & Gilbert W. Taylor* 2.00
_____YOU CAN LEARN TO RELAX *Dr. Samuel Gutwirth* 2.00

HOBBIES

_____BLACKSTONE'S SECRETS OF MAGIC *Harry Blackstone* 2.00
_____COIN COLLECTING FOR BEGINNERS *Burton Hobson & Fred Reinfeld* 2.00
_____400 FASCINATING MAGIC TRICKS YOU CAN DO *Howard Thurston* 2.00
_____GOULD'S GOLD & SILVER GUIDE TO COINS *Maurice Gould* 2.00
_____HARMONICA PLAYING FOR FUN & PROFIT *Hal Leighton* 2.00
_____JUGGLING MADE EASY *Rudolf Dittrich* 1.00
_____MAGIC MADE EASY *Byron Wels* 2.00
_____SEW SIMPLY, SEW RIGHT *Mini Rhea & F. Leighton* 2.00
_____STAMP COLLECTING FOR BEGINNERS *Burton Hobson* 2.00
_____STAMP COLLECTING FOR FUN & PROFIT *Frank Cetin* 1.00

HYPNOTISM

_____ADVANCED TECHNIQUES OF HYPNOSIS *Melvin Powers* 1.00
_____ANIMAL HYPNOSIS *Dr. F. A. Völgyesi* 2.00
_____CHILDBIRTH WITH HYPNOSIS *William S. Kroger, M.D.* 2.00
_____HOW TO SOLVE YOUR SEX PROBLEMS
   WITH SELF-HYPNOSIS *Frank S. Caprio, M.D.* 2.00
_____HOW TO STOP SMOKING THRU SELF-HYPNOSIS *Leslie M. LeCron* 2.00
_____HOW TO USE AUTO-SUGGESTION EFFECTIVELY *John Duckworth* 2.00
_____HOW YOU CAN BOWL BETTER USING SELF-HYPNOSIS *Jack Heise* 2.00
_____HOW YOU CAN PLAY BETTER GOLF USING SELF-HYPNOSIS *Heise* 2.00
_____HYPNOSIS AND SELF-HYPNOSIS *Bernard Hollander, M.D.* 2.00
_____HYPNOSIS IN ATHLETICS *Wilfred M. Mitchell, Ph.D.* 2.00
_____HYPNOTISM *(Originally published in 1893) Carl Sextus* 3.00
_____HYPNOTISM & PSYCHIC PHENOMENA *Simeon Edmunds* 2.00
_____HYPNOTISM MADE EASY *Dr. Ralph Winn* 2.00
_____HYPNOTISM MADE PRACTICAL *Louis Orton* 2.00
_____HYPNOTISM REVEALED *Melvin Powers* 1.00
_____HYPNOTISM TODAY *Leslie LeCron & Jean Bordeaux, Ph.D.* 2.00
_____HYPNOTIST'S CASE BOOK *Alex Erskine* 1.00
_____MEDICAL HYPNOSIS HANDBOOK *Drs. Van Pelt, Ambrose, Newbold* 2.00
_____MODERN HYPNOSIS *Lesley Kuhn & Salvatore Russo, Ph.D.* 3.00
_____NEW CONCEPTS OF HYPNOSIS *Bernard C. Gindes, M.D.* 3.00
_____POST-HYPNOTIC INSTRUCTIONS *Arnold Furst* 2.00
   How to give post-hypnotic suggestions for therapeutic purposes.
_____PRACTICAL GUIDE TO SELF-HYPNOSIS *Melvin Powers* 2.00
_____PRACTICAL HYPNOTISM *Philip Magonet, M.D.* 1.00
_____SECRETS OF HYPNOTISM *S. J. Van Pelt, M.D.* 2.00

_____SELF-HYPNOSIS *Paul Adams*		2.00
_____SELF-HYPNOSIS Its Theory, Technique & Application *Melvin Powers*		2.00
_____SELF-HYPNOSIS A Conditioned-Response Technique *Laurance Sparks*		2.00
_____THERAPY THROUGH HYPNOSIS *edited by Raphael H. Rhodes*		3.00

JUDAICA

_____HOW TO LIVE A RICHER & FULLER LIFE *Rabbi Edgar F. Magnin*	2.00
_____MODERN ISRAEL *Lily Edelman*	2.00
_____OUR JEWISH HERITAGE *Rabbi Alfred Wolf & Joseph Gaer*	2.00
_____ROMANCE OF HASSIDISM *Jacob S. Minkin*	2.50
_____SERVICE OF THE HEART *Evelyn Garfield, Ph.D.*	2.50
_____STORY OF ISRAEL IN COINS *Jean & Maurice Gould*	2.00
_____STORY OF ISRAEL IN STAMPS *Maxim & Gabriel Shamir*	1.00
_____TONGUE OF THE PROPHETS *Robert St. John*	3.00
_____TREASURY OF COMFORT *edited by Rabbi Sidney Greenberg*	2.00
_____TREASURY OF THE ART OF LIVING *edited by Rabbi S. Greenberg*	2.00

MARRIAGE, SEX & PARENTHOOD

_____ABILITY TO LOVE *Dr. Allan Fromme*	2.00
_____ENCYCLOPEDIA OF MODERN SEX & LOVE TECHNIQUES *R. Macandrew*	2.00
_____GUIDE TO SUCCESSFUL MARRIAGE *Drs. Albert Ellis & Robert Harper*	3.00
_____HOW TO RAISE AN EMOTIONALLY HEALTHY, HAPPY CHILD *Albert Ellis, Ph.D.*	2.00
_____IMPOTENCE & FRIGIDITY *Edwin W. Hirsch, M.D.*	2.00
_____NEW APPROACHES TO SEX IN MARRIAGE *John E. Eichenlaub, M.D.*	2.00
_____PSYCHOSOMATIC GYNECOLOGY *William S. Kroger, M.D.*	10.00
_____SEX WITHOUT GUILT *Albert Ellis, Ph.D.*	2.00
_____SEXUALLY ADEQUATE FEMALE *Frank S. Caprio, M.D.*	2.00
_____SEXUALLY ADEQUATE MALE *Frank S. Caprio, M.D.*	2.00
_____YOUR FIRST YEAR OF MARRIAGE *Dr. Tom McGinnis*	2.00
_____BOOK OF TALISMANS, AMULETS & ZODIACAL GEMS *William Pavitt*	3.00
_____CONCENTRATION—A Guide to Mental Mastery *Mouni Sadhu*	2.00
_____DREAMS & OMENS REVEALED *Fred Gettings*	2.00
_____EXTRASENSORY PERCEPTION *Simeon Edmunds*	2.00
_____FORTUNE TELLING WITH CARDS *P. Foli*	2.00
_____HANDWRITING ANALYSIS MADE EASY *John Marley*	2.00
_____HANDWRITING TELLS *Nadya Olyanova*	3.00
_____HOW TO UNDERSTAND YOUR DREAMS *Geoffrey A. Dudley*	2.00
_____ILLUSTRATED YOGA *William Zorn*	2.00
_____MAGICIAN — His training and work *W. E. Butler*	2.00
_____MEDITATION *Mouni Sadhu*	3.00
_____MENTAL TELEPATHY EXPLAINED *Hereward Carrington*	.50
_____MODERN NUMEROLOGY *Morris C. Goodman*	2.00
_____NUMEROLOGY—ITS FACTS AND SECRETS *Ariel Yvon Taylor*	2.00
_____PALMISTRY MADE EASY *Fred Gettings*	2.00
_____PALMISTRY MADE PRACTICAL *Elizabeth Daniels Squire*	2.00
_____PALMISTRY SECRETS REVEALED *Henry Frith*	2.00
_____PRACTICAL YOGA *Ernest Wood*	2.00
_____PROPHECY IN OUR TIME *Martin Ebon*	2.50
_____PSYCHOLOGY OF HANDWRITING *Nadya Olyanova*	2.00
_____SEEING INTO THE FUTURE *Harvey Day*	2.00
_____SEX & HUMAN BEHAVIOR BY THE NUMBERS *Alexandra Kayhle*	2.00
_____SUPERSTITION — Are you superstitious? *Eric Maple*	2.00
_____TAROT *Mouni Sadhu*	3.00
_____TAROT OF THE BOHEMIANS *Papus*	3.00
_____TEST YOUR ESP *Martin Ebon*	2.00
_____WAYS TO SELF-REALIZATION *Mouni Sadhu*	2.00
_____WITCHCRAFT, MAGIC & OCCULTISM—A Fascinating History *W. B. Crow*	3.00
_____WITCHCRAFT — THE SIXTH SENSE *Justine Glass*	2.00
_____WORLD OF PSYCHIC RESEARCH *Hereward Carrington*	2.00
_____YOU CAN ANALYZE HANDWRITING *Robert Holder*	2.00

SELF-HELP & INSPIRATIONAL

_____ACT YOUR WAY TO SUCCESSFUL LIVING *Neil & Margaret Rau*	2.00
_____CYBERNETICS WITHIN US *Y. Saparina*	3.00
_____DOCTOR PSYCHO-CYBERNETICS *Maxwell Maltz, M.D.*	2.50
_____DYNAMIC THINKING *Melvin Powers*	1.00
_____GREATEST POWER IN THE UNIVERSE *U. S. Andersen*	4.00
_____GROW RICH WHILE YOU SLEEP *Ben Sweetland*	2.00
_____GUIDE TO DEVELOPING YOUR POTENTIAL *Herbert A. Otto, Ph.D.*	3.00
_____GUIDE TO HAPPINESS *Dr. Maxwell S. Cagan*	2.00
_____GUIDE TO LIVING IN BALANCE *Frank S. Caprio, M.D.*	2.00
_____GUIDE TO RATIONAL LIVING *Albert Ellis, Ph.D. & R. Harper, Ph.D.*	2.00
_____HELPING YOURSELF WITH APPLIED PSYCHOLOGY *R. Henderson*	2.00
_____HELPING YOURSELF WITH PSYCHIATRY *Frank S. Caprio, M.D.*	2.00
_____HOW TO ATTRACT GOOD LUCK *A. H. Z. Carr*	2.00
_____HOW TO CONTROL YOUR DESTINY *Norvell*	2.00
_____HOW TO DEVELOP A WINNING PERSONALITY *Martin Panzer*	2.00
_____HOW TO DEVELOP AN EXCEPTIONAL MEMORY *Young and Gibson*	2.00
_____HOW TO OVERCOME YOUR FEARS *M. P. Leahy, M.D.*	2.00
_____HOW YOU CAN HAVE CONFIDENCE AND POWER *Les Giblin*	2.00
_____I WILL *Ben Sweetland*	2.00
_____LEFT-HANDED PEOPLE *Michael Barsley*	3.00
_____MAGIC IN YOUR MIND *U. S. Andersen*	2.00
_____MAGIC OF THINKING BIG *Dr. David J. Schwartz*	2.00
_____MAGIC POWER OF YOUR MIND *Walter M. Germain*	2.00
_____MASTER KEYS TO SUCCESS, POPULARITY & PRESTIGE *C. W. Bailey*	2.00
_____MENTAL POWER THRU SLEEP SUGGESTION *Melvin Powers*	1.00
_____ORIENTAL SECRETS OF GRACEFUL LIVING *Boye De Mente*	1.00
_____PSYCHO-CYBERNETICS *Maxwell Maltz, M.D.*	2.00
_____SECRET OF SECRETS *U. S. Andersen*	3.00
_____SELF-CONFIDENCE THROUGH SELF-ANALYSIS *E. Oakley*	1.00
_____STUTTERING AND WHAT YOU CAN DO ABOUT IT *W. Johnson, Ph.D.*	2.00
_____SUCCESS-CYBERNETICS *U. S. Andersen*	2.00
_____10 DAYS TO A GREAT NEW LIFE *William E. Edwards*	2.00
_____THINK AND GROW RICH *Napoleon Hill*	2.00
_____THREE MAGIC WORDS *U. S. Andersen*	3.00
_____YOU ARE NOT THE TARGET *Laura Huxley*	3.00
_____YOUR SUBCONSCIOUS POWER *Charles M. Simmons*	2.00
_____YOUR THOUGHTS CAN CHANGE YOUR LIFE *Donald Curtis*	2.00

SPORTS

_____ARCHERY — An Expert's Guide *Don Stamp*	2.00
_____BICYCLING FOR FUN AND GOOD HEALTH *Kenneth E. Luther*	2.00
_____COMPLETE GUIDE TO FISHING *Vlad Evanoff*	2.00
_____HOW TO BEAT BETTER TENNIS PLAYERS *Loring Fiske*	3.00
_____HOW TO WIN AT POCKET BILLIARDS *Edward D. Knuchell*	2.00
_____HOW TO WIN AT THE RACES *Sam (The Genius) Lewin*	2.00
_____MOTORCYCLING FOR BEGINNERS *I. G. Edmonds*	2.00
_____PRACTICAL BOATING *W. S. Kals*	3.00
_____PSYCH YOURSELF TO BETTER TENNIS *Dr. Walter A. Luszki*	2.00
_____SECRET OF BOWLING STRIKES *Dawson Taylor*	2.00
_____SECRET OF PERFECT PUTTING *Horton Smith & Dawson Taylor*	2.00
_____SECRET WHY FISH BITE *James Westman*	2.00
_____TABLE TENNIS MADE EASY *Johnny Leach*	2.00
_____TENNIS MADE EASY *Joel Brecheen*	2.00

WILSHIRE MINIATURE LIBRARY (4¼" x 6" in full color)

_____BUTTERFLIES	2.50
_____INTRODUCTION TO MINERALS	2.50
_____LIPIZZANERS & THE SPANISH RIDING SCHOOL	2.50
_____PRECIOUS STONES AND PEARLS	2.50
_____SKIER'S POCKET BOOK	2.50

WILSHIRE HORSE LOVERS' LIBRARY

Notes

Notes

Notes

Notes

Notes

Notes

Notes

Notes

Notes

Notes

Notes